Philosophy in the Mass Age

When George Grant delivered *Philosophy in the Mass Age* over the CBC radio network early in 1958, it was an immediate hit. He criticized the Western notion of progress and affirmed the role of philosophy in teaching and assisting people in understanding. Robert Fulford described it then as stunningly effective: 'Grant's talks, obviously the product of a supple and curious mind, were models of their type – learned but clear, original but persuasive, highly personal but intensely communicative.'

Grant's analysis of the paradox of modernity is no less intriguing today. The need to reconcile freedom with the moral law 'of which we do not take the measure, but by which we are measured and defined' is still an issue in our times.

William Christian has restored the text of the original 1959 edition. He has supplemented it with material from the broadcast version of the lectures, including a ninth lecture, not previously published, in which Grant responded to listeners' questions. The controversial introduction to the 1966 edition appears as an appendix.

WILLIAM CHRISTIAN is the author of *George Grant: A Biography*, and a professor in the Department of Political Studies, University of Guelph.

GEORGE GRANT

Philosophy in the Mass Age

Edited with an Introduction
by William Christian

UNIVERSITY OF TORONTO PRESS
Toronto Buffalo London

© University of Toronto Press Incorporated 1995
Toronto Buffalo London
Printed in Canada

ISBN 0-8020-0438-5 (cloth)
ISBN 0-8020-7228-3 (paper)

Originally published by the Copp Clark Publishing Company 1959;
reprinted 1966

Printed on acid-free paper

Canadian Cataloguing in Publication Data

Grant, George, 1918–1988
Philosophy in the mass age

Revision of 8 lectures originally broadcast in Jan.–Feb. 1958
in the radio series CBC University of the air and transcription
of Grant's answers to questions in a 9th program, Mar. 10, 1958.
Reprint of main texts originally published in 1959 & 1966 by
Copp Clark, Toronto.
Includes bibliographical references.
ISBN 0-8020-0438-5 (bound) ISBN 0-8020-7228-3 (pbk.)

1. Civilization, Modern. 2. Ethics – History – 20th century.
3. Philosophy, Canada. I. Christian, William, 1945– .
II. Title.

CB358.G73 1995 191 C94-932779-4

University of Toronto Press acknowledges the financial assistance to its
publishing program of the Canada Council and the Ontario Arts Council.

Contents

Contents   vi

Editor's Introduction

When the Canadian Broadcasting Corporation approached George Grant in 1957 to deliver a series of lectures on philosophy to a national radio audience, he had been teaching at Dalhousie University for a decade. Almost from his arrival in Halifax he established himself as a formidable intellectual presence, and he quickly charmed and fascinated both the large number of students who enrolled in his first year philosophy class, as well as a smaller group who idolized him and followed him to the senior level courses.

Concern for education was a family legacy. Both his grandfathers were farm boys who became important figures in educational circles. His mother's father, Sir George Parkin, was the founding secretary for the Rhodes scholarships, a post he held from 1902 until his retirement in 1920. Grant's paternal grandfather, George Monro Grant, was principal of Queen's University in Kingston, Ontario from 1877 until his death in 1902.

Although Grant's grandfathers had been important figures, their grandson was still little known. Born two days after the Armistice, on 13 November 1918, Grant was educated at Upper Canada College, where his father was principal. He then enrolled at Queen's, where he took his four-year honours degree in three years, and still managed to win the history medal and a prestigious Rhodes scholarship. In spite of Canada's declaration of war against Hitler in September 1939, he decided to take up his award at Oxford, and spent the academic year 1939–40 studying law. During that year, Grant was increasingly torn by two rival impulses. He was under fierce pressure from his family to do his duty to King and Country; they wanted him to enlist in the armed forces. However, he had strongly inclined to pacifism as a teenager and undergraduate, and the influence of the friends he made at Balliol College, Oxford, reinforced his determination not to contribute actively to the war effort. He decided instead to volunteer for the unpaid post of Air Raid Precaution warden in Bermondsey, a working class district of south London.

That year changed his life. Bermondsey was one of the most heavily bombed areas of London, and the destruction of historic buildings and the death of so many of his friends took a heavy emotional and physical toll on the twenty-two-year-old. After the bombing of London, he decided to join the Merchant Marine, but was found to have a tubercular lesion, a serious, often fatal disease at the time. Panicking, he disappeared, and worked for a while as a farm labourer. When the news came that the Japanese had bombed Pearl Harbor, he was close to suicide.

A few days later, however, he was riding his bicycle down a road to begin farm work. He got off his bike to open a gate across the road. By the time he walked his bike through and closed the gate, he knew for a certainty that God existed. This moment was the defining moment of his life. For the rest of his life, he tried to make intellectual sense of this primal experience. *Philosophy in the Mass Age* was his first extensive attempt to address the theological and philosophical problems that arose from that vision of eternity.

Most philosophers write for other philosophers first, and only incidently for the ordinary reader. Grant was unusual, in that his writings often originated in a spoken and public form. He learned to be a public philosopher after he had returned to Toronto and his mother had nursed him back to emotional and physical health. For the last two years of the war, he worked for the Canadian Association of Adult Education (CAAE) and, as national secretary, was responsible for organizing the Citizens' Forum radio broadcasts, an important early experiment in using national radio for adult education. After the war he returned to Oxford to study theology and began a D.Phil. thesis on the Scottish Calvinist theologian John Oman. In 1946 the University of Toronto offered him the post of warden of Hart House. However, the offer was a controversial one and encountered resistance. Governors who objected to the fact that Grant had been a pacifist for the first two years of the war blocked his appointment.

He was at the centre of another controversy in 1951 and 1952. He had been requested to write a study on philosophy in English Canada for the royal commission on culture headed by his uncle, Vincent Massey. Most academic philosophers greeted his report with hostility. According to B.K. Sandwell, the distinguished journalist and editor of *Saturday Night*:

> It was not, however, Mr. Grant's views about the two P's [pragmatism and positivism] that stirred up the hornet's nest; it was his general denunciation of the philosophy departments of the Canadian universities (other than the Roman Catholic ones) for not doing their job, his crediting of other university departments with most of the best current philosophical writing, his definition of the task of philosophy as the 'analysis of the traditions of our society and the judgment of those traditions against our varying intuitions of the Perfection of God', and finally his denunciation of 'the dream of philosophy – that it might free itself from its traditional dependence upon the theological dogmas of faith,' a dream that he says Canadian philosophers have shared with the rest of the western world.[1]

Throughout the 1950s he appeared on radio and television from time to time. He was a frequent guest on *Fighting Words* and he continued to support the adult education movement by speaking to conferences and contributing to broadcasts. On 9 November 1955 he delivered an important radio lecture on the French existentialist philosopher Jean-Paul Sartre for the CBC's *Architects of Modern Thought* series. The lucid and elegant talk, which explored Sartre's understanding of human beings as radically free, made a strong impression on listeners.[2]

Although hardly an important media figure, Grant was sufficiently experienced in broadcasting that, when the CBC decided to initiate a university of the air, Lewis Miller, a former student of his at Dalhousie, could argue a persuasive case that Grant had both the personality and strength of intellect to make philosophy accessible to a national radio audience. Starting on 1 January 1958, Grant broadcast eight lectures, one each Monday, followed by a ninth on 10 March 1958, in which he responded to listeners' questions.

The lectures were a triumph and instantly established Grant as an important thinker. Rex Williams of Copp Clark thought so highly of them that he approached Grant and arranged for their publication. When the lectures were published as *Philosophy in the Mass Age* the next year, in 1959, the book confirmed the original impression. Robert Fulford, one of Grant's first admirers outside the academic community, reviewed it in the Toronto *Star*. He praised the radio lectures as 'stunningly effective.' For him, 'Grant's talks, obviously the product of a supple and curious mind, were models of their type – learned but clear, original but persuasive, highly personal but intensely communicative.' Although the published version lost 'Grant's marvellous radio personality,' the compensation was a chance to absorb his ideas more slowly and carefully.[3] Co-publication in the United States was also a modest success. Sydney Harris, a columnist for the Chicago *Daily News* called it an unsatisfying book for those looking for answers to fundamental questions, but a useful one for those looking for the fundamental questions themselves. He thought that its one hundred pages contained 'enough suggestive material for a dozen books.' Grant, he said, was 'worried and confused – and his book asks us to share his concerns and address ourselves to the ultimate problems of man's nature and destiny.'[4]

Grant was normally a slow and careful worker. He did not easily achieve the lucid and elegant prose that characterizes his work. He often meditated on ideas for years before he felt sufficiently confident to express his thoughts in writing. Had he not already been thinking the matter through for some time, he could not have prepared *Philosophy in the Mass Age* so quickly.

Indeed, he had begun work on a book in 1956, during a sabbatical leave spent in England with his family. Throughout the year he jotted his thoughts down in a notebook.[5] 'What is my book going to be about?' he asked himself. 'Start out with the American spirit. What is good & what is bad in it? The questions that arise therefrom.'[6] This focus on the United States was not something new in his thought. He was twenty-two when he wrote a letter to his mother from Bermondsey in 1941 saying that

European civilization has been greater than ours is now – but we have the promise – we have the future – for us there is hope and there isn't much hope here. I agree with all these people, Europeans and Americans, who say to me America has nothing like Europe. American culture has its basis and its traditions in Europe but my answer must be: 'All right but if its traditions & basis are with you, its hope, its power to grow and the glory that it will finally bring forth will be something new built upon itself out of that land.'[7]

Now he reaffirmed this perspective in his notebook: 'Even

Hegel saw the United States "as the land of the future where the burden of world history shall reveal itself."[8]

Grant had been drawn to the nineteenth century German philosopher G.W.F. Hegel in part by his acquaintance with Oxford philosopher Michael Foster, but more through his friendship with his closest intellectual friend at Dalhousie, James Doull, a brilliant, but little-known, classicist and Hegelian philosopher. It was Hegel's concept of a philosophy of history which interested him, the notion that there was an inner logic that drove the historical process.

One of Hegel's most famous aphorisms was that the owl of Minerva only took its flight at twilight. For Grant, we were now into the twilight of European civilization and that of the United States was destined to replace it. However, it was not yet clear what the new North American civilization would be like when its full character emerged, and there were disturbing signs. It would be something prodigious and something novel. Would it be a society in which human beings could live good lives?

George Grant was a Christian, although hardly an orthodox one, and his belief in the existence of a transcendent reality lay at the core of his thought. When he talked about religion, though, he usually had in mind a social, rather than a metaphysical, phenomenon. From personal experience and from his thinking about North America, he concluded that a new religion had arisen that had replaced the older Christian tradition. This was the religion of progress, which he also called the religion of mastery, whose aim, he explained to his radio listeners, was 'the domination of man over nature through knowledge and its application' (p. 5). It was a religion in two important senses. First, it bound the society together, because it was so widely believed. Second, it gave meaning to people's lives. Its impact was all the greater in North America, because only that society had 'no history of its own before the age of progress, and we have built here the society that incarnates more than any other the values and principles of the age of progress' (p. 4).

He had first begun to theorize about the new social phenomenon in 1954 as 'the expanding economy,'[9] but he quickly concluded that this focus was too narrow. The next year he expanded his analysis to encompass the application of technology in the form of the terrible new weapons of mass destruction, and spoke of 'the atomic age.'[10] But even this characterization was partial. Any satisfactory analysis, he now understood, must reveal how comprehensive the new way of living had become. He announced this new formulation in his first lecture: 'Ours is the world of mass production and its techniques, of standardized consumption and standardized education, of wholesale entertainment and almost wholesale medicine. We are formed by this new environment at all the moments of our work and leisure – that is, in our total lives' (p. 5).

In the second and third lectures he turned to an examination of the older world view, which was being superseded by the new. Following Mircea Eliade, a professor of comparative religion whom he much admired, he described the earliest vision as a 'mythic consciousness'; that is, human acts had meaning to the extent that they repeated or participated in some divine act. This understanding of human life was given its highest formulation by Plato, who rose beyond myth to philosophy. For Plato, time was 'the moving image of eternity.' By this formulation he affirmed that the transitory events of this life had meaning only to the extent that they led human beings to 'the unchanging reality of God.'

Later thinkers in the Christian tradition, such as St Thomas Aquinas, concluded that the affirmation of the existence of a transcendent divinity permitted the derivation of a theory of natural law. Human reason can discover the order of the universe and human beings can choose to bring themselves into harmony with it. This natural law is not something we have made, yet it is binding on all human beings at all times and in all places. It tells us that there are some things that it is never right to do, whether or not it suits our convenience to do them.

The fourth lecture told the story of the decline of the older moral consciousness as an effective force shaping the moral consciousness of modern Europe. Although the doctrine of natural law dominated in Catholic Europe for centuries, its hold was first challenged by thinkers such as Machiavelli and Hobbes, and in the eighteenth century (the period we call the Enlightenment) it was subjected to prolonged and fierce attack. However, one of the most powerful attacks on natural law came not from the secularizing opponents of religion, but from such devout Christians as Luther and Calvin, and their assaults drew strength from no less an authority than the Bible itself. Because the version of Christianity that became dominant in North America was Calvinism, Grant argued that the subsequent history of North America could not be understood unless its unique dependency on biblical religion were fully grasped.

The dynamic nature of contemporary western culture had its origins, Grant suggested, in the Jewish discovery of the idea of history as expressed in the Old Testament. For the Jewish prophets, God was a personality who ceaselessly intervened in history. History was the record of those acts God had willed, but, since God did not act randomly, the prophets inferred that there was a final end or purpose towards which all His acts were directed. Time, for them, was the medium in which God's will manifested itself. The Christian doctrine of the Trinity made this view of time as history central to Western civilization. To us, 'the sense of the unique importance of historical events was made absolute by the Incarnation. Our redemption has been achieved once and for all in His passion and death' (p. 56).

In the following three lectures, Grant traced the mutation of the European spirit into the outlook that constitutes the mod-

ern vision. He saw the link between the two in the idea that
the redemption of humanity was a unique historical event.
This observation about the importance of the idea of history
brought Grant, strangely, to Marx, whose philosophy, he
observed in his notebook, was a 'farrago, but one of great
power.'[11] While on sabbatical leave in England, Grant had
read Herbert Marcuse, and he accepted Marcuse's general
interpretation of Marx. The Marx they both admired was not
the author of *Das Kapital*, whose ideas had been simplified
and rigidified by the Russian communists. Like Marcuse,
Grant esteemed Marx's earlier philosophical writings and
found in them a Marx who was 'a liberal who understood biblical religion.'[12]

Grant saw Marx as an important thinker in a process, which
began with Kant, that secularized the teachings of Judaism
and Christianity, and turned them into the form of religion
acceptable in the modern world, namely ideology. '"Philosophers have hitherto interpreted the world in various ways; the
thing is to change it." This is what my book is going to be
about. For whereas Hegel had preached the eternal recurrence
of his dialectical process, Marx by inserting the process in
time, represented history as soon about to come to an end.'[13]
Marx was, in Grant's word, a great 'cosmological' thinker.[14]
Yet, Grant's attitude to Marx was, at its heart, fundamentally
hostile. Although Grant thought that he could learn from him,
ultimately he wanted to destroy marxism 'by an appeal to the
transcendent – the mysteries.'[15]

Marx thought that it was necessary to move beyond Christianity, Grant argued, because he concluded that this religion
had never fully understood the implications of its own doctrine of the Incarnation. Marx believed that scarcity could be
overcome and that therefore the ideal of the God-man, rather
than a unique occurrence, could extend to all humanity. Freed
from its other-worldly associations, he argued, this ideal could
be realized in the world. The suffering of the proletariat, in

this reading of Marx, replaced the suffering of Christ as the instrument for the redemption of humanity. Marxism, then, was a great theodicy. It gave meaning to the affliction of the world because it taught that such suffering led ultimately to a society in which suffering was finally overcome. Marxism, understood in this sense, was 'the most influential humanist religion the world has ever known' (p. 61).

Marxism had succeeded in the East, in Russia and China, but not in the West. Why? Although Grant believed that marxism drew on powerful elements from the Western theological tradition grounded in biblical religion, he did not think that it was, ultimately, a satisfactory transformation of the whole truth of the Western moral tradition. Its failure was that it did 'not allow sufficient place to the freedom of the spirit' (p. 63). Man was a historical being, but he was also a free being, and freedom in this sense meant that man was more than an object in the world (as the dominant strain of marxist materialism treated him). He was a subject, an 'I,' someone who was always a project to himself, who could always ask the point of it all, the purpose of his existence. Marxism was, therefore, radically incomplete, yet Marx's thought had exposed a profound problem, 'a dilemma of intensity and depth' (p. 90). Traditional natural law morality accepted the existence of an unchanging human nature, but marxism, building on biblical religion, had brought that presupposition into question. Human freedom seemed to reach its apex only when human beings understood themselves, rather than God, as the makers of history.

He became aware of the importance of the subjective understanding of freedom during his early years at Dalhousie, when he studied and taught the writings of the eighteenth-century German philosopher Immanuel Kant. Kant, he believed, had played the central role in the formation of the modern understanding of morality. After Kant, it had been very hard for Western philosophers to accept morality as something given from the outside. Only moral laws we legislated for ourselves seemed to us authentic expressions of morality; morality was something that had to originate from within the individual, from a 'good will.' Because of the influence of Kant's thought, it was difficult, perhaps impossible, for most moderns to acknowledge the absolute claim of a natural law in whose making we had played no part.

We were faced with a formal dilemma. For man to be the master-maker of his own history, it was necessary to reject the moral teachings of the natural law tradition. However, our best moral sense retained a residual belief that we live within an order we do not make for ourselves, one that tells us that there are some things that we must never do; therefore, we cannot be the completely free makers of our own history. For Grant, 'The question thoughtful people must ask themselves is whether the progressive spirit is going to hold within itself any conception of spiritual law and freedom; or whether our history-making spirit will degenerate into a rudderless desire for domination on the part of our élites, and aimless pleasure seeking among the masses. Can the achievements of the age of progress be placed at the service of a human freedom that finds itself completed and not denied by a spiritual order?' (p. 69).

The word 'philosophy' in its Greek origins meant 'the love of wisdom,' and wisdom meant knowledge of how to live one's life. For Grant, there was no point to philosophy unless it led to this kind of knowledge: 'Only those will be interested in philosophy who realize that as we sow in theory so will we reap in action' (p. 95–6). It was not the philosopher's task, however, to legislate for society as a whole, or 'to speak in detail about how the contradictions of the world will be overcome in the temporal process: for instance, to predict what is going to happen in North America' (p. 69–70).

Rather, the philosopher's task was to address those moral problems that we might meet as individuals: 'Is there anything that we should never under any circumstances do to another human being? Is there a point in the degradation of a human being where we can say that so to degrade for whatever purpose is categorically wrong?' (p. 71–2). Grant's sense that it was increasingly difficult to answer these questions in North America led him to examine the character of American morality.

The single most important fact about North America, in Grant's view, was that it was formed by a religious faith that had never predominated for long in any European country, namely Calvinist Protestantism. Calvin believed in a Hidden God, by whose inscrutable Will human beings were elected to salvation or damnation. Following the German sociologist Max Weber, to whose understanding of Calvinism Grant was deeply indebted, he concluded that this belief led to an enormous practical orientation of Calvinists in the world. 'One could only contemplate God in Jesus Christ, and go out and act as best one could. It is this tradition of acting for the best in the world that has been of so influential in creating our modern North American practicality. When freed from all theological context, it becomes pragmatism' (p. 78).

Philosophical pragmatism, as expressed by American thinkers such as William James and John Dewey, had attracted Grant during the Second World War. He had even gone so far as to describe them late in 1941 as his 'favourite philosophers.'[16] However, his experience with the Canadian Association of Adult Education in 1943–5 had led him to revise his judgment, and he became an increasingly bitter critic of the theory of progressive education created from their theories. In 1955 he had delivered a brilliant attack on the notion that the role of education was to adjust students to their society in an address 'The Paradox of Democratic Education.'[17] Now the seventh of his broadcast lectures, 'American Morality' sought to demonstrate just how dangerous such an educational theory was in the circumstances of North America. Although some details of this controversy might seem dated, its central concerns still raise key questions for many modern educational theorists. Grant found the idea of education as adjustment inadequate on two grounds. As he said: '(1) A philosophy that exalts action and life over thought cannot condemn any action as categorically wrong. (2) Any philosophy that cannot condemn certain actions as categorically wrong is in my opinion iniquitous (and I choose the adjective advisedly), whatever else it may say about anything' (p. 85).

His final lecture was not a conclusion. Rather it refined the dilemma that all thinking people in North America faced. Grant had written in his notebook: 'I never seem to doubt Christianity when I get down to it – so why not admit that to thought.'[18] He now acknowledged in his radio lectures: 'I never doubt that some actions can be known to be categorically wrong.' He came down, then, on the side of the law, 'an unconditional authority of which we do not take the measure, but by which we ourselves are measured and defined' (p. 93). In turbulent times, in times of such grave uncertainty as ours, it was better to err on the side of the law or limit than in the direction of unlimited freedom.

This, however, was an ideological, rather than a philosophical, choice. Although 'the truth of conservatism is the truth of order and limit, both in social and personal life,' in Canada this stance was morally ambiguous because 'it is almost impossible to express the truth of conservatism in our society without seeming to justify our present capitalism.'

Conservatism in our present circumstances was at best a holding operation to prevent matters from getting worse. The overwhelming task for all North Americans was to rethink the doctrine of God, and to do this 'a multitude of philosophers' will be necessary, who will attend above all to the greatest question, 'the true conception of nature and its relation to history' (p. 102). Whether this rethinking will take place 'in our particular civilization cannot be determined' (p. 103).

The hesitancy in the last lecture, grounded in an awareness

of the comprehensive rethinking of the philosophical foundations of Western society that was required, was balanced
against the more hopeful conclusion of the first lecture. There
Grant had noted that the very banality of education in North
America was drawing the best students to philosophy and theology. 'And these young people are the evidence that in our
society profound philosophical thought is arising. They herald
what may yet be, surprisingly, the dawn of the age of reason
in North America' (p. 13).

For a brief period after he delivered these lectures, Grant
believed that the possibility of this renewal was imminent. As
he wrote to his friend Derek Bedson: 'I think we are in North
America at a stage where new and vital images have to come
from God to man and that I want to open myself to these new
images as they are given.'[19] He briefly, but seriously, considered the possibility that he should leave Canada so that he
could live in a place where the character of modern North
America would be fully manifest, and he investigated the possibility of a job at Claremont College in California. As he
explained to Bedson: 'I think [Nova Scotia] has many fewer
potentialities for evil and many fewer for good than California. The question for me is, Should the believing Christian
live outside the modern world (at its most modern) or in it? I
am still undecided.'[20]

There is no doubt, however, that Grant's hope for the possibility of a future reconciliation of freedom and the moral law,
and the possibility that some hint might be given in a society,
like California, where freedom had been most developed, had
its basis in Hegel's philosophy of history. His return to south-
ern Ontario, where he taught at McMaster University in
Hamilton from 1961 until 1980, was in part motivated by his
desire to live where he could experience the full force of technological society.

But he began to question the adequacy of the Hegelian synthesis when the distinguished University of Toronto Hegel

scholar Emil Fackenheim introduced him to the writings of the German-American philosopher Leo Strauss. 'I count it a high blessing to have been acquainted with this man's thought,' Grant acknowledged in the new introduction to *Philosophy in the Mass Age* when it was reprinted in 1966.

The most immediate effect of reading Strauss was to persuade Grant that he had been wrong in holding out any hope that the tensions of modernity might be resolved as freedom became more fully developed in the world. The decisive text, included in Strauss's 1959 collection of essays, *What is Political Philosophy?*, concerned his dispute with the French Hegelian Alexandre Kojève. Kojève's *Introduction à la lecture de Hegel*, based on lectures he had delivered in Paris between 1933 and 1939, had been first published in 1947. There was no gentle British idealism about Kojève's interpretation, but a brilliant, systematic elucidation of Hegel's *Phenomenology of Spirit*. Kojève's Hegel was an atheist who pointed towards the culmination of the development of freedom. The goal towards which Hegelian history was moving, according to Kojève, was a worldwide state in which there would no longer be class warfare. He called this endpoint of human history the universal and homogeneous state.

Grant's new introduction to the 1966 edition was really more like a reconsideration or a recantation. In it he declared that he had changed his mind about Hegel and that he now accepted, partly through Strauss's influence, that 'Plato's account of what constitutes human excellence and the possibility of its realization in the world is more valid than that of Hegel.' These remarks about Hegel have caused considerable controversy about the extent and nature of Grant's indebtedness to Hegel in the 1950s.

On that subject it is perhaps safest to say that, in the introduction to the second edition, Grant exaggerates the extent to which he was initially indebted to Hegel. As he had previously treated Sartre (whom he had first praised excessively and subsequently rejected with scorn), he now treated Hegel. The truth is that even while he was still at Dalhousie, Plato, St Augustine, Kant, and Simone Weil were certainly more important influences on his thought than Hegel. He had never been really happy with Hegel's theology. 'An Hegelian God just doesn't interest me,' he wrote in his notebook in 1956.[21] 'What I always feel about Hegelianism is that I have been gypped. Is this really the only hope theology has?'[22] Twenty years later, in 1977 or 1978, he reflected on his interest in Hegelianism and recalled: 'It was Hegel's doctrine of the cunning of reason – wars and stagnant pools – that drove me out of Hegelianism.' Perhaps reading Simone Weil more intensely, as he began to do in 1958, added depth to his understanding of Plato and confirmed his suspicions of Hegel's inadequacy.

However, he had found in Hegel a powerful tool to explain the process that led to the creation of the modern world. And Marx's adaptation of the Hegelian system threw even more light on the working out of modernity as a secular, progressive faith. In a 1966 review of Jacques Ellul's *The Technological Society*, Grant reaffirmed the importance of Hegel's account of how the modern West had come into existence: 'Nobody has ever seen this with greater clarity than Hegel in the *Phenomenology*.'[23] And the indirect influence of Hegel's thought is clear from the fact that Grant continued for many years to make use of the Kojèvian-Hegelian concept of the universal and homogeneous state.

George Grant died in 1988 and therefore did not live to see the fall of communism. That event would not have forced him to drastically revise his conclusions, since he often quoted with approval Martin Heidegger's observation that capitalism and communism were both predicates of the subject technology. He might very well have taken the disappearance of marxism, with its residual belief in a human teleology, as one further step towards the globalization of technology. It is reasonable to speculate that he would have agreed with Francis

Fukuyama (*The End of History and the Last Man* [1992]) that the world had moved closer to a universal and homogeneous state, but the prospect would have sent a shiver up his spine. As he had written in 1981: 'If tyranny is to come in North America, it will come cosily and on cat's feet. It will come with the denial of the rights of the unborn and of the aged, the denial of the rights of the mentally retarded, the insane and the economically less privileged. In fact, it will come with the denial of rights to all those who cannot defend themselves. It will come in the name of the cost-benefit analysis of human life.'[40]

William Christian
Guelph, Ontario
June 1994

Note on the Text

Grant delivered 'Philosophy in the Mass Age' in a series of radio lectures on the CBC and revised the text for publication. The main text reprinted here is the text of the published versions: *Philosophy in the Mass Age* (Toronto: Copp Clark 1959, 1966). I have not attempted to indicate all the changes that Grant made between the radio and printed versions. However, I have included in square brackets [ ] some additional or alternative material from the broadcast version. The text has also been rendered in University of Toronto Press house style, with minor changes in punctuation, et cetera. According to context, words such as 'man' and 'he' should be understood to be inclusive. I did not think it appropriate to make such alterations to the published text.

I have also added transcriptions of Grant's answers to questions in a ninth program after 'Philosophy in the Mass Age.' The new introduction that Grant wrote for the 1966 printing of *Philosophy in the Mass Age* appears after the text of that work, rather than before, as it did in the second edition. What Grant calls an introduction is really more like a reconsideration. It is better read in the order in which it was written. The preface that follows is the version that originally appeared in 1959 and was dropped from the 1966 reprint.

Acknowledgments

Erica Lamacraft did a fine job entering the text and transcribing the tape of Grant's answers to his listeners. Mark Haslett, with his customary efficiency and affability, gave generous advice and provided me with a transcript of the original broadcast version of 'Philosophy in the Mass Age.' Rex Williams, who originally arranged that the text of these lectures be published, was again instrumental in suggesting that they be made available in printed form. Sheila Grant, as always, was kindness itself, and gave me many helpful suggestions about both the text and the introduction. My sons, Matthew and Adam, have been very tolerant of their father's continuing interest in George Grant. I am grateful to them for their patience. I would also like to thank Barbara Christian who, as copy-editor, made sensitive and thoughtful suggestions which improved the introduction.

Preface to the First Edition

The following essays were originally spoken as an introduction to moral philosophy for a general radio audience. They must therefore be read in that light. Their introductory character means that they are in no sense a systematic treatise on moral philosophy. This must be stated explicitly because of the belief widely prevalent in North America that moral issues do not require much reflection (let alone systematic reflection) and that therefore the good life is in no way dependent upon sustained philosophical thought. Moral truth is considered to be a few loosely defined platitudes that any man of common sense can grasp easily without the discipline of reflection. The result is that moral philosophy has come to be identified with vague uplift. I would not wish that the popular form of these essays should do anything to encourage such nonsense. They are simply an introduction, intended to encourage further study.

The essays are also limited by their historical approach. I have tried to describe briefly some of the more important aspects of tradition that go to make up modern thinking on this subject. The danger of approaching moral philosophy via history is that some readers may believe that a relativism is thereby implied; that because different people at different times have made differing moral judgments, there are no true judgments that can be made in this field. No such implication can properly be drawn from what follows. I believe there is such a study as moral judgments. I have used an historical approach despite its dangers because any by-passing of history inclines to even greater dangers. Any non-historical approach may tend towards an easy dogmatism. If one were to introduce moral philosophy by analysing its concepts outside any historical perspective, one would be apt to make certain assumptions that might not be clear either to oneself or one's readers. For instance, most contemporary English writers on ethics analyse ethical concepts with great clarity and precision, but within the assumptions of the educated liberalism they hold dear. These liberal assumptions may be true but are not immediately self-evident. Many educated men have denied them and given careful reasons for that denial. To start from history may free us from this kind of dogmatism, be it liberal or of some other form. It can help us to know that certain truths we hope to be self-evident may be only the passing assumptions of a particular race or class. It is indeed true that philosophy stands or falls by its claim to transcend history, but that transcending can only be authentic when it has passed through the forge of historical discipline. It is for this reason that I have introduced moral philosophy historically and socially.

Lastly, and most important, it will be clear that I have assumed from the first sentence of these essays that there is such a study as moral philosophy, and that by reflection we can come to make true judgments as to how we ought to act. It will seem strange to those who know something of modern philosophy that at no point do I discuss this assumption, although it is generally denied throughout the sophisticated philosophical circles of the English-speaking world. For instance, the very distinction between the words 'ethics' and 'morals,' which is widely accepted in those circles, implies the denial of the assumption that I make throughout these essays. Within this distinction, 'morals' is the word applied to the whole sphere of actions that men call right and wrong. 'Ethics' is the analysis of the language of morals. The assumption is made that philosophers qua philosophers are concerned with ethics not with morals. The philosopher is concerned with using language systematically in this area of life; he is not concerned with knowing what it is to act rightly. This last activity (if it exists at all) is not the vocation of the philosopher, but of the priest or prophet. This position is not only popular among modern philosophers but is one of the most important assumptions of our educated middle-class world. In what follows I do not make this assumption. I would assert that philosophic reflection can lead us to make true judgments about right action.

Contemplation can teach us the knowledge of God's law. But in what follows I make no effort to argue directly this view of the relation between reflection and action, to justify the existence of moral philosophy. To do so would require a technical and systematic exposition that could only be addressed to persons already thoroughly conversant with the philosophic tradition. It would be out of place as an introduction to moral philosophy to a general audience; it is wrong to spend the whole time proving that there is such a study. It has always seemed to me a source of amusement as well as regret that at our leading English-speaking universities, the professors of moral philosophy spend their time proving that there is really no such subject for them to profess.

As married people will understand, anything true in what follows comes from my wife.

G.P. Grant
Halifax, Nova Scotia
May, 1959

Philosophy in the Mass Age

1

Philosophy in the Mass Society

Whereas animals live by instinct and therefore do what they do directly, we can decide between alternatives, and this choice is possible because we can reflect on how we are going to act. We can formulate general rules or principles that serve as guides among the innumerable possibilities open to us and that give some degree of consistency to our lives as a whole. Thus men who make the pursuit of wealth the chief activity of their lives have, at least to some degree, formulated the principle that all their actions will be as much as possible subordinated to that end. But also we know that how we do live is not always how we ought to live. It therefore becomes of supreme importance that we think deeply as to what are the right principles by which we should direct our lives. Through the ages the thinking about such principles has been called 'moral philosophy.' Morality is the whole sphere of actions to which we can apply the categories [of] right and wrong. Moral philosophy is the attempt by reflection to make true judgments as to whether actions are right or wrong. The making of such judgments requires knowledge of the principles of right, and knowledge to apply those principles to our particular situation.

The process of thinking through our lives in this way is of

course something that each person can only do for himself. As Luther once said, 'A man must do his own believing as he must do his own dying.' There is, however, value in discourse on the subject, particularly in considering what men have thought about these matters through the ages. Our minds are not separate, and we move towards the truth only as we are willing to learn from the full weight of what the thought of the past and the present have to tell us. Humanity has been called an inherited deposit, and we only become fully human as we make that deposit our own.

The historical situation of the West, and of Canadians in particular, calls for the frankest and most critical look at the principles of right in which we put our trust. The world situation has been described so often: the existence of two rival power blocks both with instruments of total destruction, and the living in an age when we have launched on the conquest of space aided by our new technological mastery. In political and pulpit rhetoric, we hear repeated over and over that our conquest of nature has taken us to the point where we can destroy the human race. This is, indeed, an obvious cliché, but still true.

Not only this world picture makes our situation new, but also the very texture of our North American society.[1] On this continent the modern mass age has arrived as to no other people in the world. North America is the only society that has no history of its own before the age of progress, and we have built here the society that incarnates more than any other the values and principles of the age of progress. Inevitably, other cultures are moving in the same direction. In 1957 it became obvious to the world how fast the Soviet Union was moving towards the scientific society. There, a people, scientifically backward forty years ago, have so concentrated their efforts, under the direction of a great philosophic faith, marxism, that they have caught up with and in certain fields surpassed our society with its much deeper rational and scientific traditions.

So far, however, modern scientific civilization has been most extensively realized in North America. Ours is the world of mass production and its techniques, of standardized consumption and standardized education, of wholesale entertainment and almost wholesale medicine. We are formed by this new environment at all the moments of our work and leisure – that is, in our total lives.

This world finds its chief creative centre in the Great Lakes region of North America, and spreads out from there as the dominant pattern of culture which shapes the rest of the continent. The Canadian heart of it is that vast metropolis that expands along the shores of Lake Ontario, with the old city of Toronto as its heart. It is the society of the continental chain stores and the automobile empires – the agents of which spread their culture through the rest of Canada. I, for instance, live in a little peninsula on the fringes of Canada, which two generations ago had a rather simple but intelligible agricultural, commercial, and military culture of its own. Even in the ten short years I have lived in Halifax, I have watched with amazement the speed with which the corporation empires have taken over this old culture and made it their own. This culture of monolithic capitalism creates the very fabric of all our lives.

Two characteristics above all distinguish this culture from others that have existed. First, it is scientific; it concentrates on the domination of man over nature through knowledge and its application. This dominance of man over nature means that we can satisfy more human needs with less work than ever before in history. This characteristic of our society is generally recognized. What is less often recognized is that this society, like all others, is more than simply an expression of the relationship of man to nature; it also exemplifies a particular relationship of man to man, namely, some men's dominance over other men. All our institutions express the way in which one lot of men dedicated to certain ends impose their dominance over other men. Our society is above all the expression of the dominance that the large-scale capitalist exerts over all other persons. And what makes our modern society something new in history is the new ways that these concentrated economic, political, and military élites have of imposing social dominance over the individual. The paradox indeed is this: so great is the power that society can exert against the individual that it even subjects to dominance those very élites who seem to rule. Thus at this stage of industrial civilization, rule becomes ever more impersonal, something outside the grip of any individual. We can say, then, that ours is the society of late state capitalism. [And this mass society of late capitalism is a fairly recent phenomenon for most parts of Canada.]

This new society and its intimate shaping of our lives presents to us in a particularly pressing way the need for moral philosophy. I do not mean by this anything so childish as that we can think simply about what in this culture we should accept and what reject. Individuals are not in a position where they can accept and reject their culture in this simple way and shape history by such choices alone. We cannot choose to be independent of the forces that make our mass culture far too profound simply to be thought away. The belief that the forms of society can be easily changed by our choices is a relic of the faith in liberalism, and as limited as most of that liberal faith. Philosophical faith is something rather different. Its hope is more indirect. As we live in these conditions of mass culture, we come to recognize them as profoundly new and this newness forces us to try to understand what they mean. We ask what it is that man has created in this new society. And as we try to see what we are, there arises an ultimate question about human nature and destiny. And such questions are what philosophy is. What I mean by philosophy arising out of such a situation is that so totally new is our situation in history, that we are driven to try and redefine the meaning of human history itself – the meaning of our own lives and of all lives in general. The fixed points of meaning have so disappeared that we must seek to redefine what our fixed points of meaning are. From this reassessment the shaping of our society will ultimately proceed.

The most remarkable of modern philosophers, Hegel, expressed this by saying, 'The owl of Minerva only takes its flight at twilight.' What he means is that human beings only pursue philosophy, a rigorous and consistent attempt to think the meaning of existence, when an old system of meaning is coming to the end of its day. He does not imply in the remark any ultimate pessimism, for pessimism is by definition always vain. He does not imply that philosophy only arises when it is too late. Too late for what? What he means is that we take thought about the meaning of our lives when an old system of meaning has disappeared with an old society, and when we recognize that the new society that is coming to be raises new questions that cannot be understood within the old system.

It is certain that in Canada our old systems of meaning, which suited the world of a pioneering, agricultural society with small commercial centres, have disappeared with the world they suited. And the more that people live in the new mass society, the more they are aware that the old systems of meaning no longer hold them, and the less they are able to see any relation between the old faiths and the practical business of living. For instance, the firm old Protestantism with its clear appeal to the Bible as the source of meaning, honestly and directly held the large part of English-speaking Canada a hundred years ago. It no longer does so. The mass of people no longer find in it that unambiguous meaning within which they can live their lives. This is truer than it was a generation ago; it is truer this year than it was last year. How many of the old-type, firm, and unequivocal Protestants can be found, outside certain rural areas and apart from the older generation?

Of the Roman Catholic tradition I know much less, nor do I know how much certainty its members find in its ancient wisdom. It has always been a minority tradition in North American society, outside French-speaking Canada. And I, for one, am certain that a people who have passed through Protestantism can never go back to a traditional Catholicism.[2]

I am not here concerned with the truth or falsity of Christianity nor with the question of what loyalty men should grant to established religious organizations. To say that a particular system of meaning that arose from a particular form of Christianity no longer holds men's minds is not to identify Christianity with that particular form and therefore to brand it as inadequate. What Jesus Christ did is not ultimately dependent on its interpretations. What I am saying is simply that we cannot rest in old systems of meaning. Always in human history at periods of great change, when in that change the most sensitive feel the most deeply insecure, there has been the tendency to seek an answer to that insecurity by turning to the certainties of the past. Therapies that turn back the wheel of history are proposed as remedies for that insecurity. Such reactionary experiments are always vain. In a period when meaning has become obscure, or to use other language, when God seems absent, the search must be for a new authentic meaning that includes within itself the new conditions that make that search necessary. It must be a philosophical and theological search.

Yet, as soon as we have admitted the need for that search, we must admit that our very society exerts a terrible pressure to hold us from that search. Every instrument of mass culture is a pressure alienating the individual from himself as a free being. [These tendencies have often been described in recent years by philosophers and sociologists in such books as David Riesman's *The Lonely Crowd*. In my opinion they have been most profoundly described in a book called *Eros and Civilization* by Herbert Marcuse.] In late capitalism the individual finds more and more that responsibility for his own life lies not with himself but with the whole system. Work is after all a necessity for civilization and work is always organized in an economic apparatus. And our economic apparatus is increasingly rationalized: work is more and more divided into specialized functions. In this situation the individual becomes (whether on the assembly line, in the office, or in the department store) an object to be administered by scientific efficiency experts. The human being is made to feel that he can best get along if he adjusts his attitudes to suit the collective institutions that dominate his life. Most of us know the power of these collective institutions and what they do to a person who will not conform to their demands.

This is not only true of our work but of our leisure. Modern culture, through the movies, newspapers, and television, through commercialized recreation and popular advertising, forces the individual into the service of the capitalist system around him. As has been said so often, in the popular television programs the American entertainment industry reproduces the hackneyed scenes of family life as the source of amusement. The American family (though made more prosperous than the ordinary family so that the acquisitive desire will be aroused) is described and exalted in its life, which is so perfectly adjusted to the world of life insurance, teen-age dating, and the supermarket. This, of course, glorifies our society as it is. Here is the way all decent Americans live and here is the way all mankind should live. And this exaltation helps to entrap us in the very reality described, helps us to accept our world and its system. Entertainment is used to keep people happy by identifying life as it is with life as it ought to be. Art is used to enfold us in the acceptance of what we are, not as the instrument of a truth beyond us.

In the same way, religion is no longer an appeal to the transcendent and the infinite potentiality of the spirit. It is valued as something that holds society together and helps to adjust the individual to accept the organization as it is. The fact that a reliable member of society is seen as a church-goer becomes a motive for church attendance. Advertisements are put out: 'Take your children to church and make them good citizens.' The ideal minister is the active democratic organizer who keeps the church running as a home of social cohesion and 'positive thinking.' Thus even the church is brought to serve the interests of the apparatus persuading the individual into conformity with its ends. All this, of course, makes it difficult for the individual in our society to see any point to that rational reassessment of life that I have called moral philosophy. The very system exerts pressure at every point against such an assessment.

What must be stressed in this connection is that reason itself is thought of simply as an instrument. It is to be used for the control of nature and the adjustment of the masses to what is required of them by the commercial society. This instrumentalist view of reason is itself one of the chief influences in making our society what it is; but, equally, our society increasingly forces on its members this view of reason. It is impossible to say which comes first, this idea of reason or the mass society. They are interdependent. Thought that does not serve the interests of the economic apparatus or some established group in society is sneered at as 'academic.' The old idea that 'the truth shall make you free,' that is, the view of reason as the way in which we discover the meaning of our lives and make that meaning our own, has almost entirely disappeared. In place of it we have substituted the idea of reason as a subjective tool, helping us in production, in the guidance of the masses, and in the maintenance of our power against rival empires. People educate themselves to get dominance over nature and over other men. Thus, scientific reason is what we mean by reason. This is why in the human field, reason comes ever more to be thought of as social science, particularly psychology in its practical sense. We study practical psychology in order to learn how other people's minds work so that we can control them, and this study of psychology comes less and less to serve its proper end, which is individual therapy.

This view of reason has found its most popular formulation in North America, in the philosophy known as pragmatism, famous in the writings of William James and John Dewey. This is not surprising, for it is in North America that control over nature and social adjustment has reached its most explicit development. Later on I wish to speak of pragmatism in detail as an important modern philosophy. At the moment I simply wish to emphasize that this philosophy, with its view of reason as an instrument, mirrors the actual life of our continent, in which individual freedom is subordinate to conformity.

Such an account of reason goes so deep into the modern consciousness that any other account is very difficult for a modern man to understand at all. Therefore, only by constant and relentless reflection on this modern idea can we hope to liberate ourselves from the naïve acceptance of it. Yet obviously the philosophic enterprise is only possible insofar as we have liberated ourselves from this view of reason.

Yet, as soon as one has considered the obstacles that society puts in the way of philosophic thought, one must assert the opposite, and express optimism about the possibility of philosophy in our society. Whatever else the industrial civilization may have done, it has eliminated the excuse of scarcity. Always before in history, the mass of men had to give most of their energy to sheer, hard work because of the fact of scarcity. The conquest of nature by man through technology means human energy is liberated to attain objectives beyond those practically necessary. As this becomes ever more realized, vast numbers of men are able to devote their time to the free play of their individual faculties. The constraints once justified by the fact of scarcity can no longer in North America be justified on those grounds. Always before in history, if some few men were to be able to pursue the life of philosophy, it depended on the labour of others, who because of that labour, were themselves removed from the possibility of the philosophic life. The ideal of human freedom the philosophers held up was always denied by their dependence upon the work of others. Such a contradiction becomes increasingly unnecessary. Reason, considered as domination over nature, has freed man from his enslavement to nature so that it is open to him to pursue the life of reason as more than simply domination. The world of mass production and consumption and the idea of social equality makes this possible. Whatever we may say against our society, we must never forget that.

Indeed, just as our industrial civilization creates the conditions of repression, it also creates the natural conditions of universal liberation: not only in the economic sense that people who are free from the necessity of hard work have the leisure to pursue ends beyond the practical, but also in the sense that an industrial society breaks down the old natural forms of human existence in which people traditionally found the meaning for their lives. In such a situation many persons are driven by the absence of these traditional forms to seek a meaning that will be their own.

Anybody who sees much of the young people of our big cities will know what I mean. They are freed from the pressing demands of scarcity at the same time as they are freed from the old framework of tradition. And this produces in them a state of high self-consciousness; they are immensely open to both good and evil. This does not mean simply that the end of scarcity makes possible a high level of self-consciousness to nearly all classes in society. A more subtle process is implied. However much the repressive elements of late industrial society may lie on us like chains, this very society is a fruit of the civilization of Europe: the civilization of rational theology, of the Reformation, and of the Enlightenment, a civilization that brought men a knowledge of themselves as free as had no other in the past. And these young people, whether they know it or not, hold in their very being the remnants of that tradition, the knowledge of themselves in their freedom, even if much else from that tradition has never been theirs. Thus knowing themselves as free, they know their freedom as standing against the pressures of the society that bind them in an impersonal grip. In such a society the best of them are open to the philosophic life with an intensity worthy of the greatest periods of human thought. How this happens is concretely expressed in the novels of J.D. Salinger. In the *New Yorker* of May 1956, Salinger had a story called 'Zooey,' which describes just such people. One finds them among the youth wherever one goes in North America. God reigns and the salt cannot lose its savour.

What is sad about these young people is that our educational institutions cannot be ready to meet their needs. Our educational institutions at all levels are still largely formed by what is most banal in our society. They have lost what was best in the old European education. They are spiritually formed by the narrow practicality of techniques; they are immediately governed by ill-educated capitalists of narrow interest. But this very failure of our educational institutions is part of that alienation that will drive the best of our students to philosophy and theology. And these young people are the evidence that in our society profound philosophical thought is arising. They herald what may yet be, surprisingly, the dawn of the age of reason in North America.

2

The Mythic and Modern Consciousness

How we act depends on what we consider life to be about, what we think is going on in human history in general, and in our own lives in particular. We do what we ultimately think is worth doing because of our vision of human existence. There is of course a great difference among people in the degree to which their vision is thought out explicitly, and the extent to which it merely lies in the root of their personality dominating their lives half-consciously. Emerson said, 'What you do speaks so loud, I can't hear what you say,' meaning that in our actions we expose the central core of ourselves and that central core is our vision. 'By their fruits you shall know them.'

It is immensely difficult to become aware of our own world picture, both because it is so deeply assumed as to be almost our very self, and also because at this point the dependence of the individual upon the structures of society is at its most powerful. Individual beliefs as to the nature and destiny of man make, and are made by, the forms of society. The proposition that the individual makes society is as much a half-truth as its converse. It requires, therefore, vigorous acts of intellect and will if the individual is to stand apart and judge what truth

there is in his own vision and in the visions of his society. To
make a true judgment about a world view is to pass beyond it.
And, as the world picture is almost identical with the self, the
act of philosophy is not only a continual negation of the self, a
continual self-transcendence; it is often, also, a negation of
what is most dear to one's own society.

An aid in understanding our assumptions is to compare
them with those that men have held in other cultures. I therefore will compare modern man's conception of his existence
with the vision of the traditional religious cultures. There is a
radical gulf between these two visions, and as we define that
gulf, we come to understand what modern man does assume,
and how these assumptions have not always been necessary.
In describing the difference, I must be allowed to use specific
and even technical terms, the meaning of which will only be
clarified gradually.

The most characteristic belief of modern man is that history
is consciously and voluntarily made by human beings. This is
what I mean by saying that modern man is 'historical' man.
He believes that the chief purpose of life is the making of history. This assumption appears so evident that it seems simply
a truism. Yet it sharply distinguishes us from the peoples of
ancient cultures. They did not believe that human beings make
history and therefore did not see themselves as 'historical'
men shaping unique events. They saw human life in a quite
different way. They saw events as the pale shadows of divine
realities, the temporal as the mere image of the eternal. Therefore, they did not see themselves as making events but as living out divinely established patterns.[1]

[Obviously this older belief of traditional religious societies
is immensely alien to us in North America, for with us the
idea of man as the practical maker of history is more completely realized than in any other society. As I have said before,
North Americans have no history before the age of progress
and therefore the denial of history and of progress in ancient

societies appears especially foreign to us. Therefore I must describe this view in some detail.]

To give these generalizations any content, it is necessary to state what is meant by ancient man and ancient cultures. The main distinction is between modern scientific culture and all societies that existed before the age of progress, both primitive societies and the ancient civilizations of Europe, Asia, and America. But this second class obviously includes immense differences. There is clearly a qualitative distinction between the mythic consciousness of early peasant societies and the high ancient civilizations. Another distinction must be made between the ancient civilizations and western European civilization before the age of progress. Though in medieval Europe there is much that seems similar to the old cultures, modern scholarship has amply demonstrated that the foundations of modern scientific culture were already emerging in the twelfth and thirteenth centuries, so that there was clearly a new element in Europe, absent in the ancient cultures. Yet, as soon as one has distinguished primitive consciousness from the ancient civilizations, it must be remembered that the latter arose from the former, and the old ways continued to exist in the new. In the fine flowering of Greek civilization in the fifth century BC, with all its efforts to transcend the mythic consciousness, one is aware that it is from the primitive culture that this civilization came.

It is also necessary to emphasize within these ancient cultures the difference between those whose beliefs were explicit and those who with less self-consciousness continued in their archaic mentality. As in our society, what people believed was not always formulated in clear, theoretical language. It can only be deduced from their behaviour, which is itself a symbol through which we can come to understand what they believed about existence. But we can also see the ancient beliefs, rational and illuminated, in the great philosophers of the ancient East and West. In the same way, if we look for the fundamental beliefs of modern culture, we can either look for them in the symbols and myths and rites of our age, in the moon-rocket launching sites, in the general appeals to progress, or in the religious rites with which the big three automobile companies annually unveil on television the sacred new models. Or we can see our culture when it is most explicit to itself in its philosophers such as Marx or Sartre, or at a slightly less explicit level in such thinkers as Freud or Bertrand Russell.

As far as we can see, to primitive men all important activities were sacred, that is, they were made holy by religious association.[2] The world of work, of farming and fishing and hunting, the world of leisure, of games and art and sexuality, were, for these people, rituals. A human act had meaning insofar as it was thought of as repeating or participating in some divine act that had been performed by a god in the golden age of the past, and which was given to men in myth. Thus, for instance, the act of sacrifice exactly reproduces that original act of sacrifice performed in the golden age by some god, and the particular act is meaningful to the individual because it repeats the initial archetypal sacrifice. By archetype is meant the original divine model of which all human acts are copies or imitations. Thus events are filled with the sacred and have their meaning in being so filled. Any actions that could not be given this kind of religious significance were considered profane. For events to be profane, to be unique and individual instead of repetitive and universal, was for them almost to be unreal, for it was the religious element that conferred reality. This is why when we look at primitive men, we can often see them merely as silly and superstitious. Leaving aside for the moment the right of modern man to make such judgments, we can see that these criticisms are generally made because we have no conception of events as hierophanies, that is, of events as the appearance of the sacred, or as theophanies, that is, as the appearance of the divine. And however silly the interpretation of the sacred may be in particular cases, especially in the more primitive cultures, we must recognize that it was through this vision of the world as a place for the appearance of the sacred that ancient men found meaning in their lives. The way, the truth, and the life had been laid down by the divinities *in illo tempore*. Human action was the re-creation of the sacred in the world. It is this that at its highest gives us the sense of rhythm and harmony that we feel in the lives of the ancient Greeks.[3]

At a high level of sophistication, this mythic consciousness can be seen in the great Greek plays. A few years ago the Stratford Festival in Ontario produced one of the greatest of these plays, Sophocles's *Oedipus Rex*. What made that production finally unsatisfactory to me was that it failed to catch this spirit of the ancient world. The producer did not seem to understand that Oedipus is living out in his suffering an archetypal pattern and that the particular events and actions of the play are only symbols of that mythic pattern. This failure was perhaps inevitable as the play was produced by modern men and women who judge the meaning of human life quite differently. I ought to say in passing that this example is itself ambiguous, and shows the difficulty of making clear generalizations on this subject. The Greek dramatists may not have held explicit theories as to the archetypal nature of their subject matter. We, on the other hand, have, thanks to Freud, the clearest theoretical recognition of the Oedipus legend as an archetype. This, however, in no way invalidates my central point.

In most ancient cultures the prime act of the creation of the world was reproduced every year in the religious ritual of the community. A carry over of this ancient spirit into the modern world is the way that in traditional Christian communions the liturgy follows through and repeats each year the birth, passion, death, and resurrection of Our Lord. Every day the sacrifice of Calvary is re-enacted in the mass. And among ancient people, the reproduction of the original, creative divine act was seen as the way they could recreate the eternal in their midst and so overcome the meaninglessness of existence. In this way human beings in endlessly repeated imitative acts brought back the divine into the world.

For the ancient man, justice is only the living out in time of a transcendent eternal model of justice. Law, which is the foundation of all communities, is seen first and foremost as that supreme law which pre-exists both written laws and the state itself. The application of law is not only undertaken for its own sake, nor only for its usefulness to society, but because it mirrors the eternal law. Thus the ancient religious cultures, as their premises became clear and explicit, saw the basis of their moral codes in the doctrine of natural law. In all civilizations up to the last few centuries, it has been in the doctrine of natural law that men came to know what was right and wrong in their actions. An act was right insofar as it was in conformity to the natural law, and wrong insofar as it was not.

But I must return to the fact of how alien this view of the world is to modern men. In this ancient vision, man gains his reality solely through repetition of and participation in a divine reality. To us who count our personal uniqueness as so important this emphasis must seem very strange. It means that this type of man sees his own life as meaningful only insofar as he ceases to be himself and imitates and repeats the eternal archetypal gestures of the divine, such as the creation of the world and the bringing forth of life. This must seem paradoxical to us. How can a man find meaning simply by not seeing his actions as his own?

It can be said that this ancient world view has its most luminous justification in the philosophy of Plato, in which time is considered as the moving image of an unmoving eternity and in which the passing events of life only have meaning as they lead men to the unchanging reality of God. In Plato's account of the last hours of Socrates' life, the supreme calm of the philosopher before his approaching death comes from his

knowledge that death will be the completion of his liberation
from the shadows and imaginings of the world to the reality
beyond change. 'The prisoner leaps to lose his chains.' In
Plato's *Phaedo*, the image of the prisoner in chains is exquis-
itely used to unite the two aspects of the dialogue, as an account of Socrates' death and as Plato's theory of eternity.
Socrates is the very image of salvation to the classical world.
'Philosophy is the practice of dying.' This view of reality has
been the basis of the mystical tradition that has flowered in
both East and West. In mysticism, men have sought to find
their true selves by being united with that which is beyond
change. They have believed that they could find themselves
by losing themselves in the divine.[4] When we read Plato's
Republic, we can see in the full light of day what the ancient
cultures at their highest conceived morality to be. Here the
doctrine of natural law is worked out in detail as the very
foundation of moral activity.

Yet as soon as one has said that Plato gives the fullest justification of the ancient cultures, it must also be stated that his
philosophy quite transcends the mythic consciousness that
was basic to those cultures. Here again Hegel's aphorism
about the owl of Minerva is apposite. At the height of Greek
civilization, its most remarkable philosopher illuminates the
assumptions of that civilization and in doing so passes quite
beyond these assumptions. In the *Republic* the morality and
religion of the archaic world as found in Homer and Hesiod is
made wonderfully explicit, but it is also most stringently criticized and in that criticism transcended. In Plato's doctrine of
the soul and of knowledge, human beings come to know
themselves as free, and therefore as finally outside religious
myths and images. From the ancient religions of Greece, philosophy takes its origin, but through the rational consciousness, which is philosophy, men find that there is no possibility
of resting in the mythic. To say therefore that in Plato we find
the noblest justification of mythic religion is true only if we

also insist that in his thought its inadequacy is first clearly expressed.

When we look at the people of ancient cultures, we surely must often ask ourselves how they bore the terrible vicissitudes of their lives, the enslavements, the famines, and the wars. In the catastrophes of the twentieth century, the outraged and the sensitive have also asked themselves what meaning, if any, the historical process may have. But the calamities of ancient history were in many ways more terrible than ours. Men were more helpless before pain. Yet, when one studies the ancient world, one is conscious of the tremendous meaning men found through all the terror, a meaning that was more than a mere survival value, more than a mere grim courage to bear the worst. What enabled them to achieve this sense of meaning was their assumption that historical time was not really important. They saw it simply as a vehicle through which necessity and the good played out their relation over and over again. Among the less sophisticated, the whole social apparatus of religious ritual and the images and symbols that were closely tied to their everyday world taught them to find the sacred in a vast variety of circumstances. Among the educated the belief that through philosophic knowledge the individual could partake of the divine during his life and eventually move by purification beyond the cycle of time gave purpose in the midst of uncertainty.

At this point it can be seen what is meant by calling modern man historical and by contrasting him with ancient peoples. In ancient cultures, men simply refused history. They overcame historical time by giving it no significance. For modern, historical man, time is a series of unique and irreversible events. Therefore, what happens in history is of supreme consequence. As it is of such consequence, it is of ultimate importance that we shape those events as they should be shaped. We have taken our fate into our own hands and are determined to make the world as we want it. Man and not God is the maker of history. Unique and irreversible events must be shaped by creative acts of human will.

This modern view is evident in the talk we hear these days about the hydrogen bomb and the other weapons of horror. It is said that man now has it in his power to end human history. Therefore it is said that the decisions of leading statesmen are of vast importance, because upon these decisions what happens in human history depends. Human history is considered the be-all and the end-all. But ancient man simply could not have believed this. Time ran its course through an infinite series of cycles. No event is new or unique. It has happened, happens, and will happen again. We can see this at its clearest in the speculations about time of both Greek and Indian philosophers. The most famous example of this belief in the ancient world was the popular idea that Socrates has lived and died, and will live and die an infinite number of times. Events did not happen once and for all. Suffering was therefore never final. The cycles periodically regenerated themselves. Thus, perhaps an ancient man would not be able even to admit the idea with which we are faced – that we can end human history. He could believe that one cycle had reached a low point in its degeneration, but he was certain that it would be regenerated in the endless cycles of time that mirror the eternal present.

To repeat, North Americans have no history before the age of progress, and therefore the denial of progress and of history appears especially foreign to us. The idea that we make history and that this is what is important is so completely taken for granted that we hardly think of it, let alone question it. The dominance of this spirit is seen in the activities that are considered most important in North America: those of the engineers, the businessmen, and the administrators. These are the people who are really doing something, because they are changing the world. We see it negatively in the activities that are not considered important: those of the artists, the lovers, the thinkers, and the people of prayer, for these are all activi-

- he gives no credit to anything beyond the immediate, love can change...it takes time.

ties that do not change the world. We see this spirit in the terrible sadness about old age in this continent. The old person is coming to an end of being part of history; he has probably come to an end of his ability to shape history. Old people are no longer good administrative, economic, or sexual instruments. Therefore, old age is more and more seen as an unalleviated disaster, not only by those people who are outside it but by those people who are old themselves. We sometimes treat old people kindly, but we patronize them. We do not see age as that time when the eternal can be most realized, and we therefore pity the aged as coming to the end of historic existence.

This historical spirit is of course not absolute in our society. Subtle conglomerations of belief from previous eras still continue to exist, even though we have so strongly broken with our past. In each one of us, beliefs from ancient times and from the Christian era continue to exert their influence both consciously and unconsciously, conflicting with one another and with membership in the modern world. As individuals, we can take seriously activities that are beyond history making. Twenty-five years ago the most popular crooner of the day, Bing Crosby, was singing 'I don't wantta make history, I just wantta make love.' Nevertheless, despite such a qualification, the generalization may be made that insofar as human beings are capable of believing they make history and therefore of living in the historical absolutely, the élites of North America have achieved this state.

It is only necessary to see how rocked our society was when the Russians got that piece of metal up into the sky before we did. They had beaten us at our own game and the game we consider important. So from our business and military leaders the cry goes up that we must intensify our history-making activities, we must be tougher history makers. It is of supreme importance that we beat the Russians to the moon. What has happened, of course, is that throughout the East the traditional religious societies, which had existed for much longer than those in the West, have crumbled, and Easterners have taken over the history-making spirit for themselves. They had to do this if they were not to be perpetually enslaved by Western men. And as the guide in their transformation into modern, historical men they have a great and carefully thought philosophy – marxism. Marxism is, after all, a Western philosophy, coming from that remarkable people, the Germans, and dedicated to the idea of man the creator of history. This new spirit under the banner of marxism conquers the traditional societies of Asia. And thus the historical spirit passes from being merely western to being world-wide.

Perhaps the very apotheosis of this spirit will come when man, united on this planet, sees his central purpose as pressing out farther and farther into an imperialism over space. When one listens to a man such as von Braun, the famous rocket scientist, talking with such joy about the infinite possibilities now open to us, one really sees what is meant by the modern spirit. The infinite is not the ancient eternal-beyond-time, but the limitless possibilities of men for action in space and time. Now that Western man has made his civilization worldwide, he turns outward to be the maker of worlds beyond.

Historical man has been compared with ahistorical man, whose ideas are largely alien to us; the idea of time as cycles endlessly repeated has been compared with the idea of time as a set of unique and irreversible events. The writer believes that this comparison is useful, because only as we become capable of thinking outside modern assumptions are we able to see at all what our assumptions are. In the same way, the study of the Greek philosophers such as Plato and Aristotle is wonderfully illuminating. As we try to think with them their vision of human nature and destiny, we come to see our own. In the eighteenth century it was common to speak of the quarrel between the ancients and moderns, as a way of understanding these different assumptions. This is why the dying out of careful philosophical study in Canada is one factor helping to produce our dead-level, conformist society. When people have not thought about ideas quite different from their own, they tend simply to live within the principles of their civilization, not even conscious that they are living within those limits.

I have not compared modern historical man with the ancient religious cultures in order to take sides; to imply, for instance, that the ancient cultures were better than our own. It is only necessary to think what modern men have done to make life pleasant, to cut down the curses of pain and work (and they are curses) to see how great the achievements of the modern world have been. The old, traditional societies governed by landlords and clerics required most men to spend the day at back-breaking physical work and to be a prey to disease and scarcity.

To see both the truth and inadequacy of such a conception as man the maker of history requires careful thought; I will only begin to assess the question at the end of these essays, and then only tentatively. What must first be done is (1) to see in detail how the religious civilizations formulated their beliefs philosophically into a clearly thought ethical system, i.e., the doctrine of natural law, and (2) to see the force of that doctrine. Only after we have seen its power, can we see why men gave it up and started to believe in the modern, historical morality.

3

Natural Law

The theory of natural law is the assertion that there is an order in the universe, and that right action for us human beings consists in attuning ourselves to that order. It is the most influential theory of morality in the history of the human race. We meet it in some form wherever we go among the pre-scientific civilizations: in Greece, in Rome, in India, in China, and among the European peoples up to the last two hundred years. It is still the cornerstone of the ethical theory of the Roman Catholic Church. In the present desegregation issue in the United States, it is appealed to by constitutional lawyers, in this instance, the suggestion being that men by their very nature have certain inalienable rights, irrespective of the colour of their skin. Indeed, only in the last two hundred years has it ceased to be the generally assumed theory from which moral judgment proceeds. It is popular to speak of a crisis in our standards and values. This sense of crisis arises above all from the fact that the doctrine of natural law no longer holds the minds of most modern men, and no alternative theory has its universal power. Not only are most people unaware of what natural law means, but when they learn of it, it seems somehow strange and alien to their modern perspective.

As I explained in the last chapter, the doctrine of natural law arose among men of the ancient cultures as they passed beyond their mythic beginnings and began to think of the world as an ordered universe, which their minds could understand. They began to think about this order, not only as it appeared in the planets, but also as it was exemplified in human action. In the Western world (which is our chief concern) it arose among the Greeks, who were the first to practise systematic science and philosophy. These studies presupposed that it was the nature of mind to seek that order that is manifest in the universe. The Greek formulation of natural law was taken over by the Romans as the theoretical basis of their great empire of law. The doctrine was later immensely illuminated by Christian revelation, as also on the other hand the Christian Church was illuminated by it. It passed over into European civilization through the Christian Church.

The doctrine was the following: There is an order in the universe that human reason can discover and according to which the human will must act so that it can attune itself to the universal harmony. Human beings in choosing their purposes must recognize that if these purposes are to be right, they must be those that are proper to the place mankind holds within the framework of universal law. We do not make this law, but are made to live within it. In this doctrine certain assumptions are made, first, about the universe in general and, secondly, about human beings in particular.

The assumption about the universe is that it is a cosmos and not a chaos. That is, it conforms to law; and to conform to law is to be held in being by reason. The great Roman lawyer Cicero puts this extremely well in his book *De Legibus*. 'What is more true,' he writes, 'than that no man should be so stupidly arrogant as to suppose that reason and mind are to be found in himself and not to suppose that they are to be found in heaven and earth, or to suppose that those things that are scarcely to be comprehended by the highest reason are not themselves set in motion by reason ... Since all things that have reason stand above those that are devoid of reason and since it is blasphemy to say that anything stands above the universe as a whole, we must admit that reason is inherent in the universe.'

In Cicero's statement the assumptions of natural law become clear. By law is meant not something simply human, which we make. It is that which at every point makes the universe what it is. It is that reason which is common to God and to men. The universe is a great system of beings, all moved by law and ultimately governed by the divine mind. It is a hierarchy in which all beings have their place, from the stones that obey the laws of the physical world, up through the plants and animals to man, and beyond man to the angels, and finally to God, who is reason itself. The noun 'nature' and its adjective 'natural' are other words for the order of the universe. And the nature of any particular thing is that which it is when it realizes its immanent meaning, that is, when it takes its proper place in the whole. To take an example popular in the ancient world: the laws of a beehive may be dictated by the instinct of the bees and the laws of a human state by legislation, but when the beehive or the state are what they ought to be, both types of law are an expression of reason and intelligence. They are reflections of that divine intelligence which is the ultimate arbiter of all.

This view of the universe as a great chain of being bound together by mind must be understood, if we are to see the moral principles of natural law that arise from it. Aristotle once said that the belief that there was a moral law depended ultimately on how we interpreted the movements of the stars. What he meant by this is that if we come to deny that the planets in their motion can be known as finally caused, we will eventually, if we are consistent, deny that there is any purpose or law governing human life. If we deny that, we are denying that there is such a thing as human morality.

In other words, the doctrine of natural law depends unequivocally on the existence of metaphysical knowledge. Metaphysics is the study of reality as a whole. It asserts that we can make true judgments about reality. To speak of the 'nature of man,' 'the order of the universe,' 'final causality,' or 'God,' is to speak metaphysically. Obviously, when Aristotle asserts that there is a final cause of the motion of the planets he is not giving a scientific explanation in the modern sense of that phrase. Yet only if we can affirm that there is metaphysical knowledge of this kind can we speak of natural law and deduce the principles of right action from that conception. In this sense a natural-law morality stands or falls with metaphysical knowledge. The truth of this can be seen in history from the fact that the denial by modern philosophers that there is metaphysical knowledge has gone hand in hand with the criticism of the natural-law account of morality.

Secondly, this doctrine makes certain assumptions about human beings and the way they should live. It assumes that there is a human nature and that this human nature is ultimately the same in all men. It does not depend on whether we are tall or short, black or white. This universal human nature is to be a rational creature. Our place in the hierarchy is to be distinguished from animals as being rational and from God as being creatures. With regard to human action, we have the power to determine for ourselves, through intelligence, the ends that are proper to us. This is not to deny that for the ancients reason was immanent in a stone or in an animal — both of which were thought of as expressions of the law. Man, however, has a rational soul, as distinct from an animal soul. The ends that we pursue are not given us directly in the way they are given an animal through instinct. We must discover our proper ends through reflection.

The believers in natural law saw clearly that our ability to reason about ends is not something given to us immediately. We are governed by laws that we only partly understand. Reason is at first only present in us potentially and not actually. It needs to be developed, and developed by education. Education is seen as the process by which a person comes to think clearly about the proper purposes of human life. (How different this is from our modern technical education that is simply concerned with teaching people how to get on, never with teaching them where they are getting on to.) In the old theory of education, when a man began to see what was the ultimate purpose of human life, he was said to be wise – to have the virtue of wisdom. Wisdom was then the purpose of education. It was the condition that men reached through reason, as they came to know what were the purposes in human life truly worthy of a rational soul.

To live according to nature was then the supreme good for a man, as it was for any being in the universe. But, of course, our nature being higher than that of an animal demands of us a higher way of life than that which is good for an animal. The good life for man includes within it the perfection of his rational nature. Man is to be perfected and brought to his highest possibility through the union of his reason with the divine reason. Thus, the logical completion of natural law is to pass beyond a simply practical life to a life of mysticism. Practice passes into adoration.

It is easy to see how this doctrine of natural law produced the fundamentals of our legal system. The law that is administered in the courts originates and derives its sanction from the eternal law of justice that is at one the law of God and of nature. Worldly laws, the laws of the land, depend on that supreme law that pre-exists both written laws and the state itself. As late as two hundred years ago, this was almost universally believed by practising lawyers. The great English jurist Blackstone put it with clarity: 'This law of nature being co-eval with mankind and dictated by God Himself is of course superior in obligation to any other. It is binding over the whole globe in all countries at all times. No human laws are of any validity if contrary to this and such of them as are valid derive their force and all their authority, mediately or immediately, from this original.'

The distinction between natural law and positive law was then clear. Positive laws are the laws that men enact, but they are only true laws insofar as they are in conformity with a law that is more than man-made. Cicero uses a very good simile to explain this: Suppose you go to a doctor, and he, looking very wise, writes in his unintelligible jargon what you are to drink and you take this paper to the drugstore and the druggist makes up the prescription and you drink it and find out it was poison. Was it a prescription that the doctor gave you? Yes, in a sense it was. A dose written down by a doctor to be made up by a druggist is a prescription. Yet the whole meaning and purpose of a prescription is that it should be for the advantage and healing of the patient.

This is true of laws also. A law is only a law when it is a just law, mirroring the divine law of justice. Both conservatives and radicals have appealed to this doctrine. The radical has said that existing law was not in conformity with divine law and therefore should be changed. Conservatives have said that some proposed change was turning away from the divine law and therefore wrong. But in the past both conservatives and radicals generally believed in this divine law from which they derived their judgments. Thus, for instance, the idea of a fair trial as necessary to a just system of law became part of the way we do things because it was believed that all individuals have certain rights. Those rights belong to them by the very nature of things and cannot be taken away by the whim of others, by the officials of government or by dictators, or for the convenience of democracies.

Not only in the laws of the state but also in the personal moral decisions of life was the doctrine of natural law operative. The right way to live could be deduced from that unchanging law that is the reason and will of God. Moral conduct was therefore not considered a matter of convenience, but the attempt to actualize the eternal law in one's own life. The question of abortion will serve as an illustration. More and more modern states now allow abortion in certain circumstances. This is because abortion is believed to be something that you choose to do or not to do, at your own convenience. This has not yet come officially into Canada because the old tradition about this matter still lives on. But I think it is true that more and more people believe that abortion is a permissible act and practise it when the need arises. The traditional believer in natural law would say that abortion is a wrong act, and that the wrongness of the act is not affected by whether it suits our convenience or not. It is a law of nature, which we did not make and which we cannot alter, that we should not extinguish what is at least potentially a human soul.

This is why you come across in Greek plays or in Shakespeare the idea that being a dictator or committing incest is an unnatural act. These acts are looked upon with horror because they are contrary to what is demanded from us as human beings. The Germans have a word for this that turns up in that matchless work of art, Mozart's *Magic Flute*. A dictator is called an *Unmensch*, a non-human. Dictatorship is not only wrong because it affects the convenience of other people, but also because it affects the dictator himself: to be a dictator is to fail in fulfilling one's manhood. It does not belong to the order of being a man to rule other men at one's own whim.

It is plain what a clear and powerful doctrine of morality natural law was. It gave to those who held it a sure and certain sense of direction. First and foremost, the doctrine was clear that moral standards are not relative but absolute. Right action was not considered a matter of our convenience. The objective moral law does not depend on what we think. As sophisticated a practising lawyer as Cicero said: 'Only a madman could maintain that the distinction between honourable and dishonourable, between virtue and vice is only a matter of opinion.'

Such a quotation illustrates how far many people in the modern world have departed from the doctrine of natural law. So often one hears modern people who have some education say that right and wrong are just matters of convenience or of opinion and that therefore there are no absolute moral standards. How influential this is in our society can be seen from the fact that the late Chief Justice Vinson of the United States Supreme Court could state this in a legal judgment as if it were so obvious that it did not need arguing. And those who take this view often think they have proven it when they point to the fact that people have believed different actions to be right at different times and places. Indeed, the belief that there are absolute standards of conduct is often supposed to be a very unsophisticated belief held only by simple people who do not know what the score is. After one has attended university or the cocktail parties of the prosperous, one will give it up. In Canadian history, how many people have come to university from well-defined moral backgrounds and been taught that a man, wise in natural or social science, is educated when he is a sceptic about moral questions. This used to happen more often that it does now because most people are now brought up in a world where this moral relativity has become the tradition. Indeed we are told from our earliest youth by the psychiatrists and their publicists that belief in absolute standards is positively unhealthy and will at the least lead us to difficulty in adjusting ourselves to society and at the worst will lead us to the mental hospital.

[I do not wish to discuss at this point whether there are such things as absolute moral standards of right and wrong. I will say what I think about this matter at the end of this series. But what I wish to insist on is that those who held and do now hold the doctrine of natural law did believe that there were such absolutes. And this belief was not confined to the simple, nor was it simply something that the powerful and educated tried to put over in their own interests. It was a doctrine that the most educated and sophisticated people in the ancient world honestly believed to be true. It was this that gave such particular moral clarity to so many of the great men of that world.]

The second implication of the doctrine of natural law is that reason leads us to know what is right. The good man is the reasonable man. The believer in natural law took for granted that reason could be practical. The vast range of particular desires did not appear to him simply as a chaos, because reason could present to him that idea of a highest rational good in terms of which all his desires could be brought into an intelligible and ordered system of life. The idea of the highest good was that in which not only particular desires would be satisfied but that in which the total self would find its completion, its happiness. The doctrine distinguished between happiness and pleasure. This highest good was the purpose for which life was lived and all our particular purposes should be subordinated to it. But this highest good could only be known through reflection. Therefore, the life of reason was the most important thing for the individual and for society. It was this indeed that led people to take the life of philosophy so seriously in the ancient world. If reason could be the ultimate governor of life, if the good life was the rational life, then philosophy became very important. To repeat, it was believed that a man's reason is at first only potential, and needs to be developed. The very word philosophy meant that. It was a combination of the Greek word 'philo,' meaning love, and the word 'sophia,' meaning wisdom. 'Philosophia' – the love of wisdom. Philosophy was the attempt to incarnate wisdom in our very lives. This is what Plato is saying in his *Republic*, and what Aristotle is saying in his *Ethics*.

How different is the importance granted to the life of reason in our Canadian institutions. Reason is generally thought of as an instrument. Practical reason is a means that can help us to achieve what our passions lead us to desire. But it is these desires and not reason that are considered as ultimately determinative of action. This is why reason to a North American is generally thought of as scientific reason. For scientific reason is concerned with the external and its control from human purposes. It is not concerned with what human purposes are good. This again can be so clearly seen in our educational system. Education is concerned with teaching young people techniques by which they can do things in the world. There is almost no concern in our educational system with seeing that our young people think deeply about the purposes for which these techniques should be used. Just look at the training of our engineers and scientists. Although we call the Russians materialists, we must remember that they give their young people more time in their curriculum to look at such questions than we permit our students. The question 'for what purpose?' we leave to the ministers and even more to psychiatry, the new ministry. We believe that such questions are fundamentally answered if we cultivate in young people certain emotional attitudes. Reasonable discussion of moral purposes has therefore almost entirely disappeared from our schools and universities.

It must be emphasized that the doctrine of reason as a subjective tool of our convenience is held not only by the mass of people but by the most influential philosophers of our day. As famous a philosopher as Bertrand Russell repeats over and over again that thought is not the arbiter of human action, that it has no ultimate voice in telling us what is worth doing. And of course no philosopher has had such influence over the semi-educated of the English-speaking world in the last generation.

[I have described the doctrine of natural law at such length because it looks so differently at morality from the way most of us have been trained to do.] When the doctrine of natural law is compared with modern theories about morality, one issue stands out as a central point of divergence. It is this point of divergence that I want to emphasize more than anything else in these essays. To put this issue simply: are we truly and finally responsible for shaping what happens in the world, or do we live in an order for which we are not ultimately responsible, so that the purpose of our lives is to discover and serve that order? There are philosophers (Hegel, for instance) who have claimed to include the truth of both these sides in their philosophies and thus to have reconciled this divergence. Whether or not they have succeeded is not our concern here. What matters first is to see how divergent are these ways of looking at the world and what different moralities they must lead to.

In natural law theory, it is clear that man is not finally responsible for what happens in the world. He chooses to conform or not to conform to an order that he himself does not make. But as the individual only has reality within the system, if he chooses not to conform then the order simply breaks him and brings his efforts to naught. To go against the natural law is both for society and the individual to descend into chaos and nothingness. This means that finally the individual has no choice but to accept the God-given order. The theorists of natural law use the words 'choice' and 'freedom' in a much more limited sense than that of the popular usage of the liberal West. Freedom does not mean the ability to make an unambiguous choice between open possibilities. We become free only insofar as we base our relevant actions on the law; we lose our freedom as we disregard that law. Thus in traditional Christian theory the highest stage of the good life is to be beyond choice. To be free is to be a slave. As St Augustine puts it: 'To be able not to sin is a great liberty; not to be able to sin is the greatest.' What is ultimately important to a man then is to know that he is not his own, that he is a creature who did not make himself. A modern exponent of natural law, George Macdonald, put the doctrine very clearly when he wrote: 'The first principle of hell is "I am my own."'[1]

How different is the humanist view of life. Man makes the world, and there is no overall system that determines what he makes. To act is to choose what kind of a world we want to make. In our acts we show what things we regard as valuable. We create value, we do not participate in a value already given. We make what order there is; we are not made by it. In this sense we are our own; we are independent. We are not bound by any dependence on anything more powerful than ourselves. We are authentically free because what happens in the world depends on us, not on some providence beyond our control. The fate of man is in his own hands. We and not God are the creators of history.

To put the issue in this simple way: 'Are we our own or are we not our own?' is not to imply that any kind of intelligible answer can be discovered simply or quickly. To begin to answer such a question would first require a careful analysis of such words as 'freedom,' 'law,' 'adoration,' 'the making of history,' and many others. This issue takes us to the heart of the relations between metaphysics and ethics and between religion and morality. It is with such systematic analysis and synthesis that moral philosophy is concerned. What is first necessary is to say something historical about why modern Europeans came to criticize and to reject the doctrine of natural law. Even a preliminary account of such criticism goes to the roots of the history of the Western world in the last centuries.

4

History as Progress

It has been the destiny of the western European peoples to be the first to destroy their old religious society and to replace it with modern scientific culture, something radically different from anything that existed in the past. To repeat, the fundamental difference between our modern society and the old is not only, or even primarily, the external difference shown by our mastery over nature through science and technology, but a profound difference in man's very view of himself. We no longer consider ourselves as part of a natural order and as subordinate to a divine law. We see ourselves rather as the makers of history, the makers of our own laws. We are authentically free since nothing beyond us limits what we should do.

If we are to understand ourselves, we must try to understand how this change came about, what was going on in the minds of those who criticized the old religious societies out of existence and who brought into being the new scientific society of historic man. In essays such as these the whole complex of causes that goes to make up so profound a change can only be discussed in a very general and therefore unsatisfactory way. The causes touch on the very centre of human consciousness, and the change is accomplished in the struggle and agony of many lives over many centuries. Every aspect of human life is involved in it – politics, economics, art, science, morality, and religion. The historical task is to search for the unity between what has happened in all these seemingly disparate fields: to see how the theologians affect the politicians and how the inventors affect the theologians and how the artists affect the scientists and so on. In what follows, no such proper historical description will be possible and it will be necessary to write very generally about an intricate historical problem.

To make the main point about the doctrine of progress clear I must rest in simple assertions without attempting to justify them. The danger of so skipping around the centuries is to give the impression that history is not a rigorous and subtle study. What also makes such generalizing unconvincing is that the change here described happened often without the men who were responsible for it being fully aware of the assumptions on which they acted. It is a necessary principle of any proper philosophy of history that the conscious intention of human actions is often different from the meaning of those acts as events in the historical process, considered philosophically. It is this that Hegel is describing in his doctrine of the 'cunning of reason.' For example, Luther's intention in acting the way he did at Worms obviously did not consciously include the significance that that event was to have in the history of the race. But to accept the difference between intended action and the meaning of event is to have insisted that historical explanation only completes itself within philosophy. It is to write as a philosopher of history, not simply as an empirical historian.

The most important cause of this change to man seen as the maker of history seems to me without doubt to be Christianity. Of all the points I am going to make in these essays, this is the most difficult to understand. What I am saying is that Christianity has been chiefly responsible for the destruction of the old religious cultures and the coming to be of our modern, secular culture. This must appear paradoxical, because we in

Canada identify Christianity with religion. We identify the old world with Christianity. It therefore seems contradictory to say that Christianity has been the chief cause of the destruction of the traditional religious cultures.

In support of this thesis, I want to start from one historical fact, which seems inexplicable on any other hypothesis. The modern spirit first came to be in European culture and not in the civilizations of the East. To look for the reason is to look for the radical difference between China or India and Europe. The central difference is that European civilization was, in its emergence, penetrated by Christianity. Furthermore, it can be asked what is the most important difference between the old classical world of Greece and Rome and the European society of the sixteenth and seventeenth centuries, out of which the modern spirit was to arise. It was that the classical spirit had taken into itself Biblical religion.[1] It therefore becomes essential to understand what was distinctive about this religion.

By Biblical religion, is meant the Christian interpretation of the Old Testament and its culmination in the Incarnation of God, Jesus Christ. That religion was unique in its absolute historicity. It was the Jews who discovered the very idea of history. More than anything else, what has made Western culture so dynamic is its impregnation with the Judaeo-Christian idea that history is the divinely ordained process of man's salvation. This is an idea utterly foreign to any other civilization until marxism took it to the East.

It is impossible to describe in detail the fascinating story of how the Hebrew prophets came to interpret events as directly ordered by the will of Jehovah. The God of the Jewish prophets is no longer an archaic deity who creates archetypal gestures, but a personality who ceaselessly intervenes in history and who reveals his will through particular events. The events of the world take on meaning not only as images of eternal patterns but as concrete expressions of the divine will. They therefore become valuable in themselves. What is more important, the idea of a God of will, who acts in history, brings with it the idea of a final end or purpose towards which his acts are directed, to which history itself is directed. This final end is seen as the redemption of the Jewish people through the Messiah. The events of the world come to be thought of as necessary to the final salvation of the chosen people. When the Messiah comes, the world will be saved once and for all. Thus the events of time are seen as oriented towards the future. Where for archaic civilizations 'that great day' was in the past, it becomes for the Jews something in the future. The purpose of God unfolds in the world and will culminate in his final purpose, that of redemption.

In Hebraic religion there is a new conception of God's relation to the world, a new conception of time and of the meaning of human action in time. Time no longer repeats itself endlessly as the moving image of an unmoving eternity. It becomes, rather, the vehicle of God's will. It is not infinite, but has been created by God and is moving to a glorious purpose at its end. Not a timeless eternity but the future will regenerate time, a future in which the redemptive purposes of God will be achieved. The Jews are not interested in the immortality of the individual but in the salvation of the people. The events of the world come to be thought of as unique and irreversible because they are the manifestation of a personal will.

Thus there arises from Judaic religion the idea of history, the idea that the events of human society have a meaning in their totality, as directed towards an end. We in the West so take for granted this view of history (or something derived from it) that we often forget where it came from. We think it is the way that human beings inevitably conceive the temporal process. But this view is not something that has been believed by men in all civilizations. Insofar as we believe it, we owe it above all to Hebraic religion.

This view of time as history was brought out from the narrow confines of the Jewish people into the main stream of

Western civilization by Christianity. This is what the doctrine of the Trinity is: it incorporates into the timeless God of the Greeks, the God of project and of suffering; that is, the God of love. The sense of the unique importance of historical events was made absolute by the Incarnation. Our redemption has been achieved once and for all in His passion and death. This was not going to be repeated an infinite number of times. It was a unique and irreversible event. 'His sweat was as it were great drops of blood, falling down to the ground' (Luke 22: 44). The divine Person had acted in an historic human existence. He had been lifted up and he would return again at the end of time with the salvation of the Kingdom of God.

[Salvation was not something achieved outside time, but depended on particular events in history. When for instance we hear or read in church the Revelation of St John the Divine, it seems a very strange mixture of imaginings by an early Christian about events that are going to happen in the future. But in it we can see clearly the idea of history as the sphere in which redemption will take place, that is the sphere where evil will be overcome. Human history becomes meaningful to men as the history of salvation. Utopianism enters the Western tradition through such writings.]

The idea that history is the sphere for the overcoming of evil and the hope of that overcoming has never been far from the centre of thought among those people who adopted Christianity. Throughout European history the repressed have returned again and again to this hope. It is the very foundation of the revolutionary tradition. It is the ultimate reason why Western man has taken worldly life and its arrangements so seriously. This is the truth of materialism. To God all things are possible. The material and spiritual evils of the world will yet be redeemed.

Such ideas become explicit only very slowly, at first only in the minds of the greatest thinkers and then throughout society as a whole. Among the Jewish people this vision of God as the God of history is at first confined to the prophets. The main body of the people reject this conception and are continually returning to the baser religions of their neighbours, and are only being called back to the worship of the living God, Jehovah, by the admonitions of the prophets in times of tragedy. From the beginnings of Christianity, and even to this day, Christian communities have taken into themselves elements of the anti-historical, pre-Christian religion of nature. It is indeed a fascinating study to watch the historical religion of Christianity mingling with the ancient religion of natural law in the first centuries of the Christian era. In this connection, St Augustine, the African bishop of the fifth century, is the most significant figure. In his wonderful book *De Civitate Dei*, the profoundest attempt is made to unify the religion of redemption with the philosophy of Plato. Augustine's attempt to hold these two disparate views of God and the world together may ultimately be inadequate, but it was of immense consequence for the future, as being, in outline, the spiritual basis for the wonderful civilization of medieval Europe. And at the height of that civilization, in the thirteenth century, St Thomas Aquinas synthesized the theology of natural law (with its atemporal standpoint) with the Christian conception of the God of history. His remarkable synthesis holds these two conceptions together with two theologies: a natural realm of the human reason and a revealed realm of God's mighty acts in history. This tension between the Hebraic and the Greek in Christian thought expressed itself in the practical life of the Church – in the tension between, on the one hand, the idea that the supernatural life is essentially mystical and monastic and, on the other hand, the growing desire of churchmen to influence worldly affairs for righteousness. This new, worldly spirit appears moderately within the Church in the Investiture Controversy of the eleventh century; it appears outside of the control of the organization in the ecstatic hopes of Joachim of Floris and the Franciscan spirituals and in the Utopian outbreaks that increasingly characterized the German world in the late Middle Ages.

This is no place to discuss what is true and what inadequate in the Thomist synthesis of Greek philosophy and Judaic prophecy. Suffice it to say that, in fact, the medieval synthesis was unable to hold the minds of western Europeans after the fifteenth century. And in the four hundred years since the breakdown of that balance, there has gradually arisen our worldwide scientific civilization. To use an inadequate analogy from biology: this new civilization is a unique mutation in the history of the race.

It may appear that the spirit of the modern world is the very antithesis of the religious, rooted as it is in the idea of progress rather than the idea of law, and emphasizing man's trust in his own ability to make the world rather than his trust in God. But what must be insisted is that the very spirit of progress takes its form and depends for its origin on the Judaeo-Christian idea of history. The influences shaping the modern spirit have been too diverse and subtle for any ease of intellectual relation or facile categorizing. Nevertheless, in its moral connotation there is nothing more important to its understanding than to recognize how the Christian idea of history as the divinely ordained process of salvation, culminating in the Kingdom of God, passes over into the idea of history as progress, culminating in the Kingdom of Man; how Christianity's orienting of time to a future made by the will of God becomes the futuristic spirit of progress in which events are shaped by the will of man. Only in such terms can the doctrine of progress be seen in its Utopian power and an answer be given to the inevitable question as to why the modern spirit first arose in Europe and not in the civilizations of the East.

The mediating term between history as providence and history as progress is the idea of freedom. (Call it, if you will, subjectivity.) Conscious of themselves as free, men came to believe that history could be shaped to their own ends. This consciousness of freedom appears first in the modern world in the religious freedom of the life and thought of the Reformation. As against the medieval theology of nature and supernature, in terms of which men could so marvellously take their place in an ordered cosmos, Luther insists that no man should find his proper rest in any natural images. Indeed, the Reformation may seem simply negative in that it attacks all the finite images of thought and ritual without thinking systematically of the consequences of what it has done. It protests against the idols that stand between man and God and in this sense the term Protestant is apposite. But it is more than simply protest, because it asserts that the principle of freedom must be regulative of any future theory of practice. It is more than negative in that the idea of freedom is the affirmation that the human spirit cannot be limited by any determinations. Indeed it asserts this freedom only within the religious sphere, but once it has been so asserted it cannot be confined to that sphere. In the next centuries the idea of man as free is taken into all aspects of life, into the spheres of politics, of art, and of science. For instance, Marx was to say that the overcoming of the difference between the citizen and the state, which he believed necessary to a realized democracy, was but an extension of the Reformers' overcoming of the difference between the lay and clerical orders. This extension of freedom into all spheres is justified theoretically in the eighteenth century, known therefore as the Age of Enlightenment. At the end of that century, these ideas are acted out in all their practical significance in the French Revolution.

The idea of freedom has often been expressed negatively – as in the long tradition of criticism by the middle-class European intellectuals. This criticism was man's refusal to accept any beliefs that were not his own. The old philosophical and theological tradition was attacked as clerical imposition of illusion of the freedom of the mind. The old religion was accused of having prevented man from exercising his freedom, by holding over him the idea of God – that is, of a master to whom he must be subservient. These witty criticisms of the idea of God have appeared in Europe from the eighteenth century to our own day; from Voltaire's *Candide* to Freud's *The Future of an Illusion*.

Voltaire's essay on the earthquake at Cadiz is mainly negative. It is concerned with ridiculing belief in the providential ordering of the world. How can there be a providential ordering of events when evil such as this occurs? The natural evil of an earthquake cannot be blamed on man, as can the moral evil of sin. Its cause is elsewhere. The works of God are condemned in the name of morality, so that the idea of God is killed in man's heart. Belief in God is attacked in the name of a pessimism that cannot reconcile the evil of the world with a divine purpose.

But above all, what must be made clear in this connection is that the attack on the belief in providence took place in a civilization dominated by Christian ideas about time, which held that evil would be overcome in the future. Therefore, as belief in God was driven from men's minds, it was not replaced (as it was in the classical world) by a rather sad humanism (the attempt to live life as pleasantly as one could in a meaningless world); rather, it was replaced by an optimistic humanism, by belief in progress. Time is still oriented to the future, but it is a future that will be dominated by man's activity. The idea of human freedom merges with Judaeo-Christian hope and produces the idea of progress. This means an entirely new kind of humanism. For a humanism arising in a Christian setting was bound to be quite different from one which had arisen from the archaic religious cultures. It was a humanism of project and reform. It was a humanism that put science and technology at its centre, as the means of redemption.

Thus, during the eighteenth and nineteenth centuries the idea of progress crushes the idea of providence. And in this crushing, belief in God is not now attacked on the pessimistic grounds of the evil that is present in nature and history, but on the optimistic grounds that assert human responsibility for building the Kingdom of Man – which total independence of man would be ultimately denied by any belief in a controlling power beyond the human spirit. In the name of human responsibility for alleviating evil and making the world, men came to think that belief in God was morally wrong. For belief in God was the enemy of our desire to change the world. Who was responsible for evil – God or man? [This trust in man's freedom is illustrated by a story that used to be current in the United States in the more optimistic days of the New Deal. A minister is looking at a farmer's beautiful field of wheat. The minister says: 'You should thank God for giving you such a beautiful field.' The farmer answers: 'You should have seen what it was like when He had it all to himself.' (This story is admittedly a rather flabby example of humanism.) For this spirit at its clearest and most unflinching see Albert Camus' novel *The Plague*.] The criticism of belief in God is here not negative, but rather the assertion that the claims of theology are themselves negative, because they turn men away from changing the world. The believers in progress claimed that the theologians, by deifying the spirit, put it outside the world, and in so doing assumed that the spirit cannot be actualized in the world. Bakunin, the great revolutionary, put this idea of rebellion brilliantly when he said: 'If God existed, we would have to kill him.' He meant that anything – including the idea of God – that stands in the way of man's absolute freedom to make history as he chooses must be destroyed.

Men no longer believed that they lived under a natural law that they did not make and that they had been created to obey. They came to see themselves as the makers of their own laws and values. Jeremy Bentham, the famous English reformer of the nineteenth century, ridiculed the idea of a divine law behind our human laws, because it placed events outside human control. There is no other law but that which man makes. By his conscious and voluntary acts he shapes the world, shaping it even more towards the goals of his own choice. It is this belief that in the last centuries has dominated the élites of western nations, so that today we live in a society that is the very incarnation of that spirit.

5

Marxism

In the thought of Karl Marx the meaning of the change described in the last chapter is brilliantly illuminated. Through his thought more than anyone else's, the Western spirit of progress has gone out into the countries of Asia and has become the dynamic religion of the East. Study of this thought is, therefore, pressed upon us in the West. Yet just as this understanding of marxism is most important to us, it has become most difficult, because in the last decades there has been a campaign of vilification against Marx and of suspicion of those who study his thought in any systematic manner. He has been attacked as the prophet of the worst abuses of the Soviet empire; as the subverter of the achievements of capitalism; as the enemy of godliness and morality. Although this campaign has draped itself in the flags of patriotism and of religion, it is not surprising that it has been inspired largely by those whose basic interest was the maintenance of our present property relations. [I remember when his picture was put on the cover of *Time*. The resulting misrepresentation is what we have been led to expect from *Time* when it wants to blacken a reputation. The story inside was of a jealous, half-educated, ambitious, and neurotic man driven to his hatred of capitalism by the pain from the carbuncles on his behind.] The contradictory nature of this attack stems from the mixture of fear and contempt with which it has been motivated. Why should the blackeners of Marx try to prevent systematic studying of his writings, if they consider these such a jumble of nonsense? What is especially strange in the behaviour of those who attack Marx in this wild way is that they have generally asserted their faith in God. Do they not believe then that this faith includes the belief that the truth will make men free and that therefore only in careful study can the chaff be divided from the wheat?

The contempt for Marx has not been confined to the irresponsible rich and their demagogues. It is heard from responsible business men and government officials and from their servants in the universities. This educated contempt is more dangerous to Western interests because it takes the form not of abuse but of patronizing aloofness. These people claim that the important thing is Russian and Chinese imperialism, not the spread of marxism. To those who pride themselves on their realism, marxism need not be taken more seriously than any other faith. They assert that what matters is power and not ideas. This position naturally appeals to the civil servants of Washington, London, and Ottawa who like to be considered too sophisticated in the ways of the world to take theory seriously, and believe that history is ultimately shaped by the ad hoc decisions that make up their lives. This supposed realism is, however, one-sided and short-sighted. If the word power is to mean anything, the social and ideological structure of that power must be analysed and understood. It is the pettiest view of human history to believe that the intellectuals of Asia are moved by a philosophy that is simply a tissue of wild imaginings. We must understand Marx as well as the power of Russia and of anti-colonialism if we are to understand the continued victories of communism in Asia. We must understand, indeed, how much marxism has contributed to the present political and technological power of Russian society.

It must be insisted however that Marx is worth studying not only because of his influence in the history of Asia, but also because of what he is in himself: a social theorist of the first rank, who reveals to us the diverse currents that make up the progressivist river. Indeed it must be recognized that marxism is a much profounder river than the limited canals of theory dug by the officials of the Communist party in the East or West. As has been the inevitable fate of great prophets, his disciples have consistently neglected and misinterpreted those aspects of his thought that did not serve their purposes. This process started even with his intimate friend Engels, who is inclined to interpret Marx as a disciple of Darwin. The narrowing was carried even further by such men of action as Lenin and Stalin. Marx must be studied not so much as a political-economic propagandist than as a theorist who brought together the varying streams of the humanist hope and in whose synthesis, therefore, the value of the doctrine of progress is most clearly exposed to us.[1]

Marx is essentially a philosopher of history, that is, one who believes he knows the meaning of the historical process as a whole and derives his view of right action therefrom. In a certain sense the philosophy of history is the modern equivalent of what in olden days was known as theodicy, the vindication of the divine providence in view of the existence of evil. The search for meaning becomes necessary when we are faced with evil in all its negativity. In Marx's search the starting point is the indubitable fact of evil. Reality is not as it ought to be. Men are not able to live properly, because their lives are full of starvation, exploitation, greed, the domination of one man by another. Our present society is not such that it permits men to fulfil themselves. As Marx says: 'Men are for other men objects.' No thinker ever had a more passionate hatred of the evils men inflict on each other, nor a greater yearning that such evils should cease. It is perhaps not surprising that he should have been so aware of evil, living as he did in the early years of the industrial era, when new ways of work were instituted with little respect for those who did the work. What is more surprising is how few of his contemporary intellectuals rebelled against the crimes that were being committed against working men, women, and children.

Marx proceeds from the present evil to criticism of the religious solution of that evil. He says that the religious solution is to maintain that all is really well, despite the evident evil. This solution has prevented men from dealing with the evils of the world. The idea that there is a God who is finally responsible holds men from taking their responsibility sufficiently seriously. If there is going to be pie in the sky when you die, then the evils of the world are not finally important. In this sense, religion is the opium of the people. Religion and its handmaiden, traditional philosophy, have said that reconciliation can be found in the here and now – if men will only seek God. In fact they say that evil is not what it seems and that despite it, all is well. But this is not the case: all is far from well. To pretend anything else is simply to disregard the sufferings of others. Therefore, the first function of thought must be the destruction of the idea of God in human consciousness.

As Marx wrote: 'The philosophers up to now have been concerned with understanding the world; we are concerned with changing it.' What he means is that the philosophers have sought the meaning already present. They have sought God. He is not concerned with the meaning already present, he is concerned with the creation of meaning in the future by man. He is concerned with the practical overcoming of the suffering he sees all around him. Therefore, man must take his fate into his own hands and to do that he must overcome the idea of God.

Marx's criticism of religion, however, is more profound than that of others who have said the same thing. For he recognizes that if man is to pass beyond belief in God, religion must not only be denied, but also its truth must be taken up into the humanist hope. The truth of religion for Marx was the yearning of the human spirit to overcome its evil – or, in his language, to overcome its own alienation. By 'alienation' he means that man's situation in society estranges him from the proper fulfilment of his freedom. He has never been able to live as he ought in society. Marx claims that he has freed this religious yearning for the overcoming of evil from any supernatural connotation, and shown how it will be fulfilled by man in history.

In the previous chapter, the centre of biblical thought was defined as the idea of history being the divinely ordained process of man's salvation. Marx takes over this idea of history as the sphere for the overcoming of evil. Therefore Christianity is for him the absolute religion, in that as far as religion can go, Christianity takes it. The supreme insight in Christianity, according to Marx, is the doctrine of the Incarnation, which means that God is no longer 'other' to man, because he has become man. But, according to him, Christianity had never understood the consequences of its own doctrine of the Incarnation. In a world of scarcity it could only hold the idea of 'the God-man' as an ideal once achieved, but not to be made universally concrete. It is Marx's claim that he has taken what is true in Christianity and liberated it from this limitation. He has taken the doctrine of God become man, freed it from its other-worldly associations, and shown how it can be universally realized in the time process. In denying supernatural religion, he believes that he has taken its truth into his philosophy.

Marx's philosophy of history is however not only the perfection of humanism, because it makes the religious hope serve a humanist purpose, but even more because he sees the most representative activity of the modern world, natural science, as the chief means of conquering evil. More than any other philosopher, he places the activity of the natural scientist in a setting of ethical redemption. Marx's recognition that natural science is central to the humanist hope has led many scientists to see the meaning of their activity in terms of marxism. Even today in the Western world, when many scientists do not wish or do not think it wise to espouse a systematic marxism, their real religion remains very much like it. To show this more fully, it is necessary first to describe what Marx thinks is going on in history.

This can only be understood in terms of Marx's debt to German philosophy in general and to the philosopher Hegel in particular.[2] When Marx is thinking about history, he is thinking in Hegelian terms. History is the sphere in which spirit is realizing itself in the world. It is realizing itself always in relation to nature. Here appears the distinction between spirit and nature. Nature is what it is and is not what it is not. A stone is a stone and not something else. But man is self-conscious, and self-consciousness is divided against itself. Man can always stand above himself and make himself what he is not. Every action is a project to the future, in which we negate what we are now. Therefore, man both is and is not what he is. Spirit, then, has a different logic from the logic of identity proper to nature. History is the coming to be of spirit in the world. Marx takes over this Hegelian way of thought, and limits it by finding the whole meaning of history in the relation of human freedom to nature. There is for him no nature without human significance; there is no significance to human freedom apart from the domination of nature.[3] To Marx, therefore, the way that men have organized their economic relations is the key to history. In the economic organization that expresses our relation to nature, he sees the cause of human evil in the past; in the creation of a new relation he sees the overcoming of that evil.

To state this in more detail: from the earliest days of history, men found themselves in a position of scarcity. There was just not enough food, shelter, and clothing for everybody to

have an abundance. Because of this, a society of class dominance was necessary. A minority group in society gained control of the economic life, the means of production. And as
they controlled the means upon which everybody depended
for sustaining life, they controlled society as a whole, and set
the pattern of its government, its art, its religion, its morality.
In other words, in a world of scarcity, society was necessarily
divided into classes. 'Class' in Marx is defined in a strictly
economic sense, in relation to control or lack of control over
the means of production.

This division of society has meant class struggle between
those who wanted to maintain their control over the source of
wealth and their consequent position of privilege, and the
majority, who were excluded from that control. But at the
same time as one dominant class has been imposing its control
over society through its control of the means of production,
people have also been seeking greater power over nature
through technology, and therefore introducing new forms of
social wealth. This continually changing relation of men to
nature has prevented any one class from long being able to
impose its dominance over the means of production, and so
over society as a whole. The new forms of wealth have produced new classes to challenge the power of the old rulers.
For example, in medieval society the means of production was
chiefly land, and therefore the ruling classes were the landlords. But as there came to be more and more commerce and
simple manufacturing, the new middle class arose in the new
towns. This class challenged the power of the landowners.
The times of quick and radical change in history have been
when a new class, produced by new economic conditions, has
come to sufficient power to challenge the old ruling class,
which in turn does all it can to retain its dying supremacy.

Marx also believed that as man's control over nature
becomes more complete, so the dominant classes who come to
power progressively serve a more universal interest of man-

kind. They serve the gradual emergence of freedom in the world. In the modern era it has been the historic role of the capitalists and their capitalist society to bring technology and economic organization to the point where, ideally, the conditions of scarcity might be once and for all overcome. The achievement of the capitalists has been to destroy the old natural world in which human freedom could not come to be. They have rationalized society.

At the same time, however, as capitalist society has created the conditions of liberation, it has intensified the conditions of enslavement. The very form that the ownership of the means of production takes in capitalism sharpens the class struggle to its peak. For as capitalism solidifies, it moves, because of the profit motive, to the concentration of economic control into fewer and fewer hands. The mass of mankind is cut off from control over the conditions of its own work as it is cut off from any control over the means of production. The contradiction that capitalist society creates is that it has produced the possibility of overcoming scarcity – that is, the conditions for overcoming class dominance and inequality have arrived; yet at the same time it has chained the mass of men to uncreative labour, work for which they have no responsibility. It has taken to the extreme the division between the owners of the economic apparatus and servants of that apparatus. In such a situation where liberation is possible and where alienation is actual, there can be only one result. The mass of men will not allow themselves to be excluded from the liberation that technology has now opened for them. They will take the means of production out of private control and place them under social control. They will destroy capitalism and create socialism. In this new society the basic cause of evil will be overcome. Men will no longer be for each other objects of economic exploitation. Human beings will be able to give themselves over to the free play of their faculties, to the life of love and art and thought.

The mass of people who are increasingly separated from control over their own work and over the economic apparatus as a whole, Marx calls the proletariat. Few conceptions in Marx generate so much confusion. People think that the proletariat means the hungry, the ragged, the destitute. As today in North America there are not many people who are destitute, the inference is drawn that Marx has been proven wrong about capitalism. Of course Marx hated the grinding poverty and the degrading division between physical and intellectual work that characterized the capitalism of his day. He said that industrial workers were turned into the living counterparts of a dead mechanism. But the idea of destitution is not necessary to the idea of the proletariat. The proletariat consists of those who have no creative responsibility for the society through their work, because they do not own the means of production with which they have to work. They are employees serving the private interests of their employers. For Marx, the proletariat is not one class amongst other classes, one class against other classes. It is the universal condition in which the vast majority of men find themselves in the age of the machine, when the machines and the machines that make machines serve private interests. The proletariat cannot liberate itself by producing another class society, but only by destroying the very existence of economic classes themselves. The mass of society is driven to recognize that in a machine age all work is social and rational and that therefore what must be created is an appropriate economic apparatus, not one given over to the irrational ends of private profit.

Those people who first become conscious that this is the historical position of the age will become the leaders of that liberation, the proletariat conscious-of-itself. They are the Communist party, the party that will direct the bringing in of a classless society of equality. Thus, the sufferings of the proletariat are seen as the Christian sees the passion of Christ, necessary to the redemption of mankind. It is this idea (at some level of explicitness) that has enabled countless ordinary people to endure suffering – with such high fortitude – for the sake of the Communist cause. The suffering is seen as meaningful.

It is not possible to assess here this remarkable vision of human history. There are many things to be said about it both as economic and philosophic doctrine. For instance, to assess it as an economic doctrine it would be necessary to discuss its dependence on the labour theory of value; to assess it as a philosophic doctrine, discussion of the causes of human evil would have to be introduced. Nor is it possible to describe the development of marxist doctrine in the last century or the question of how far the Russian Revolution and the consequent regime of the Soviet Union can be said to be the socialist society of which Marx was talking. It is, for instance, arguable that it is with us in North America that the conditions that Marx prophesied are most clearly fulfilled, and therefore Marx is more the prophet of North America than of Russia. These are intricate questions to which no short answer can be given.

What must be insisted on, however, is that Marx's philosophy has been the most powerful of modern humanisms, for two reasons above all. First, it was a humanism of universal salvation, and secondly, it seemed very concrete and practical about the means to that salvation. With regard to the first point: the marxist hope is not for the isolated individual but for society as a whole. His humanism is not for a few rare, fine spirits in exceptional positions, but promises the good life for all. So often humanist liberalism has been made ridiculous by its individualism that disregarded the dependence of the individual on the community, and seemed little concerned with the way the mass of men lived. But how can the human spirit find any moral fulfilment in such individualism? There can be no perfected freedom in a world where others have not found it. What kind of a heaven can be enjoyed while others are in hell?

The power of marxism has lain in the fact that it foretold a concrete overcoming of evil in the world, which would be for society as a whole. Here Marx's dependence on the Judaeo-Christian idea of history is obvious. His humanism retains the idea of history as salvation, but rejects its theological framework. This makes it incomparably more powerful than those humanisms that are liberal and individualistic.

The second reason for the power of marxism is its claimed practicality. Instead of leaving the worldly hope up in the air, it describes concretely how it is to be brought about. It relates its achievement to the forces already around us in modern society. There is much that could be said about the superiority of marxism over other doctrines of progress, on account of its direct application to the world as it is, but I will single out only one connection – the significance Marx gave to the natural scientists.

The fact to be explained is why many scientists in this century have been followers of Marx or have been deeply influenced by him. Because governments must concern themselves with treason, this fact has been surrounded with a miasma of anxiety in the last years. But the first problem is to give a serious explanation of why it has been so. The answer is surely this: marxism gave such a satisfactory account of science as essentially an ethical, indeed a redemptive activity, the means by which men were to be freed from the evils of pain and work.

Recently there was a syndicated American cartoon in our local paper. It was a drawing of a Russian commissar for foreign aid speaking to a young student whom he wishes to send abroad on a technical mission. The commissar is saying: 'I don't care about your engineering degree, what do you know of Karl Marx?' Obviously this cartoon expresses the great need the Americans have these days to keep alive their sense of superiority over the Russians. What the cartoon says is this: we Americans are interested in helping underdeveloped countries quite honestly by giving them engineers; the Russians are not really interested in helping people through engineering but in dominating them through marxism.

This is to misrepresent entirely what marxism is and the hope that men see in it. The philosophy of marxism is regarded as the guide and control under which modern techniques can be brought to underdeveloped countries, and it claims that it alone can guarantee that these modern techniques will be the servant of the good of all and not of private profit. Marx's appeal was not to the scientist as an ethical man apart from his function, but primarily in his function itself. Scientists, like other men of intelligence, want to know what purpose their activity is serving. Marx gave them a systematic answer to this question. He showed (whether accurately or not) the role of the scientific function within an optimistic and worldly philosophy of history, [a philosophy] which had a place for the universal interests of humanity.

It may be said by way of digression that it was often a contradictory tendency in Marx that made his philosophy so powerful among certain scientists. Among modern scientists there have been two ways of looking at man that have been difficult to relate. On the one hand, assumptions from geological and biological studies have led certain scientists to judge man as but a product of nature. They have believed that history is but a part of nature. On the other hand, science as technology has been obviously the victory of human freedom over nature, which means that nature has been taken up into history. Many scientists have held both these views at the same time – as theoretical men they have often asserted that their science shows that man is but a product of nature; as practical men they have asserted that science is the domination of man over nature. It may be that some scientists have been adherents of Marx because his thought seemed to hold these positions together. His materialism seemed to make man simply a part of nature; his dialectic, to make man firmly the master of nature. Thus the marxist could have the best of two worlds.

But leaving aside this digression, what is important is that marxism seemed to be tied to what was already in the world – the everyday world of technology and mass industry that surrounds us. He seemed to show men that through the present conditions of society the humanist Utopia could be achieved and progress brought to its consummation. His Utopia did not therefore seem an airy ideal, but something concrete, a possibility to be actualized in terms of what already existed. This is what has made marxism the most influential humanist religion the world has ever known. It is this that gives it its power over the East.

6

The Limits of Progress

Marxism has been described as a powerful statement of the modern progressive spirit, filled with the hope of a worldly existence freed from evil and laying down the practical steps to the achievement of that hope. It has been insisted that this is why marxism is now the dynamic religion of Asia, the chief directing force in making the progressive spirit more than European, indeed worldwide. Nevertheless, as soon as the guiding power of marxism in Asia has been stressed, another fact of modern history must also be emphasized. Official marxism has been defeated in the very civilization from which it originated. Orthodox communism has triumphed outside the social area in which marxism was conceived and for which it was designed as a social theory. Marxism claims to be the authentic product of Western intellectual and industrial development. Yet it is precisely in the West that its hold over the makers of social policy has been limited. If we are to know the truth of the modern world, we must try to understand why this has been so. To draw an analogy from another period of religious history: Buddhism was a product of India yet it was defeated in India and won its chief power in Japan and Ceylon.

The failure of orthodox communism to become the dominant faith in the West lies far deeper than in the practical arrogance and theoretical narrowness of the Party. It lies in marxism itself, even when that faith is taken at its best – in its founder. Marxism has failed in the West primarily because it does not allow sufficient place to the freedom of the spirit.[1] One is loath to say this to North Americans, because so often when marxism is attacked as denying freedom, all that is meant by freedom is the divine right of the businessman to rule society – a freedom that allows the greedy to exploit public resources for private gain. But despite the possibility of misinterpretation, I would still insist that marxism does not truly understand the freedom of the spirit. And it is for this reason that the Western peoples, at their best, have rejected it.

What is meant here may easily be confused by the varying uses of the word freedom. The word is often used to express the ability to get what we want when we want it. A rich man is free because when he wants caviar or pearls or to go to Florida, he is free to get what he wants. A dictator is free when he can get his own way with the state. This is a perfectly proper use of the word, but it is not what is meant by the freedom of the spirit. What is meant by that phrase is that man is more than simply an object in the world, he is a subject. The distinction between subject and object is obvious, yet it needs to be insisted on in a society such as ours where attention is generally focused on objects. Thinking about the world of objects is carried on by an 'I,' or subject, which is not itself an object but which is implied in all those acts of thought. The more we think about the 'I' the more mysterious this subjectivity will appear to us. On the one hand we can never escape it, it is implied in all we think and do and are. On the other hand, though we can never escape ourselves, we can never completely come upon ourselves. When we think about ourselves, we turn ourselves into an object thought about, but there is always the 'I' who is doing the thinking about the 'I.' We can think about ourselves thinking about ourselves, and we can think about ourselves thinking about ourselves thinking about ourselves. But what we really are can never become an object for ourselves. As far as action is concerned, this subjectivity implies the power to stand above ourselves and judge what we are and what we should be. We are always a project to ourselves, in that in any given situation we can negate what we are in the name of what we ought to be. We cannot therefore be explained or explain ourselves adequately in objective terms. It is this ability to transcend any worldly situation that we call the freedom of the spirit. 'Freedom' so defined is not, then, simply the ability to get what we want when we want it, but also the ability to reflect about what we should want. To use the traditional language of moral philosophy, it also implies that we cannot find our completeness in any finite object of desire.

To put it in another way: let us say that there had been achieved a socialist society in which economic exploitation of person by person had been overcome and in which there was no division between the freedom of the individual and the harmony of the whole. In such a situation a man could still ask what is the point of it all, what is the purpose of my existence. If all objective needs were satisfied, men would still not find themselves reconciled. This is in no sense to deny the value of achieving such goals or to discuss the relationship of their achievement to the achievement of our supernatural end. It is simply to say that the purpose of human life cannot adequately be defined in terms of objective goals. 'My Kingdom is not of this world.'

It is this truth that is not satisfied in marxism. In Marx's thought, the subject is finally subordinated to the object, so that it is asserted that we can find our completeness in space and time. The hope towards which marxism directs human freedom is an objective hope. The reconciliation that marxism offers man is a reconciliation in the world, not an absolute reconciliation in which the distinction between mind and world is overcome. This worldly hope is simply not adequate to our potentiality for the infinite.

This failure to take true account of human freedom affects marxism at every point, not just in the worldly Utopia that is offered man as the basis of reconciliation. To single out one point: it leads to superficiality about evil. Marxism asserts that men will live well when they are liberated from scarcity and its consequent society of class domination. Hegel saw the basic fallacy here, before Marx had expounded it. 'It is a false principle,' Hegel wrote, 'that the fetters which bind right and freedom can be broken without the emancipation of conscience – that there can be a Revolution without a Reformation.' Whatever levels of meaning this remark may have, one of them certainly is that necessary changes in the externals of society can only proceed in a community where many men already know themselves as free, and that this knowledge of freedom arises as a religious affirmation in the light of the infinite. The marxist account of freedom as depending solely on the objective situation is far too simple, because the very bringing of the objective situation to the point where its liberation is possible depends on generations of men and women having known themselves as free. This being so, Marx's account of the fetters that bind right and freedom is quite inadequate.

Indeed, the subordination of the mind to the world in marxism and the consequent superficiality of its account of evil has been responsible for that unpreparedness among marxists for the corruptions that have ravaged their own parties. Believing that scarcity and class dominance were the cause of evil, they were not ready for the demoniac outbreaks of power-seeking that have characterized the Communist worlds. Because of its superficial view of evil, there were no built-in safeguards, such as practices of spiritual purification, within the system. A phenomenon such as Stalin cannot be totally explained as a product of oriental despotism (as some Western empiricists would have it) but must also be considered as a product of marxist theory. After all, similar phenomena have appeared in all the Communist parties of the world. In another connection, this same dialectic of corruption has worked itself out among Communists because of the marxist naïvety about ends justifying the means.

This failure indicates why marxism has been officially triumphant in the East but defeated in the West. The knowledge of each person as a free subject and as of unique importance in his freedom had not been part of the old religious cultures of the East. These cultures had never passed through a stage similar to what the Reformation and the Enlightenment had meant to Europe by way of the general consciousness of right and freedom.[2] To some extent Russia was touched by the Enlightenment, but only indirectly as compared with Germany, France, or England. Therefore, when the ancient societies of the East recognized both the possibilities and the threat from the progressive European culture and realized that they were going to have to take over that culture if they were not to be slaves of the Europeans, it is not surprising that they should take over the progressive spirit in a very objective form, which did not adequately include within itself the truth of freedom. And this is marxism: a brilliant account of history that does not sufficiently recognize the truth of the spirit; a philosophy that although aware of the sins against human freedom, finally subordinates our freedom to the objective conditions of the world.

Indeed, marxism was made more suitable for Asia by the fact that revolutionary leaders such as Lenin changed Marx's thought into an ever naïver and cruder scientific materialism. [To repeat, this process is already at work in Friedrich Engels. See *Anti-Duhring*.] Darwinism had been influential in leading Engels to conceive the human spirit as dependent on the objective conditions of the world. In the thought of Lenin, the process was carried even further: the freedom of the subject was made entirely subordinate to the objective world in a way that would have been unthinkable to Marx, who saw subject and object in dialectical relationship. Certainly Lenin did not think he was misinterpreting Marx but in so doing he made marxism a more effective instrument of immediate political power. The organization of the Bolshevik party, in power and out, has always shown a ruthless subordination of the individual. Therefore it is not surprising that the party should have adopted the naïve materialism of Lenin rather than the philosophy of Marx.

After all, the origin of Marx's criticism of the capitalist system was that this system reversed the true relation between subject and object. It subordinated the worker to the conditions of his work. Thus the origin of marxism is an affirmation of human freedom, even though that freedom is not given proper theoretical place in marxism. But such an affirmation of freedom has not been much in evidence in Communist states. The workers of the East have surely been subordinated to the conditions of their work.[3] To justify this subordination, the leaders of marxism in the East turned their doctrine into a kind of simple scientism, concentrating solely on the improvement of techniques.

This can be seen in the progressive elimination from Eastern marxism of its religious undertones. As I have said, the ultimate source of marxist thought was the Judaeo-Christian idea of history as the divinely ordained process of man's salvation; therefore, Marx's doctrine of progress is filled with the ecstatic hopes of its origin. But the elimination of this ecstatic element from marxism has been necessary so that it could become official doctrine in the East. Thus it has become increasingly a species of practical materialism that excludes more and more the true significance of man in his freedom.

Nevertheless, it is the very practicality of this materialism that makes the Russians such a powerful social force at the moment. They can concentrate on definite objectives and find an immense and almost childish satisfaction in their accomplishment. And such a new thing is this practical and collectivized materialism in Asia that we can look forward to its leaders being intoxicated by such limited objectives for many generations. It is this that makes them so like Americans of the early twentieth century. Just look at Khrushchev – a tough and amusing organizer, of peasant origin, with a great zest for life, and having the most limited materialism as philosophy. What centuries of civilization separate him from a man such as Marx!

Of course eventually the Russian society will produce a new spirit of freedom. Among the children of the élites, young existentialists must be growing up who know their freedom as the negation of the world. It was heartening to read that both Russian and Chinese officials had found it necessary to condemn rock 'n' roll as a decadent occupation. Whatever the limitations of rock 'n' roll, it is an attempt of the young to express themselves on a level beyond the practical. No wonder the Russians and Chinese who want their people to concentrate their energies on immediate and collective objectives should distrust such phenomena in their midst. Indeed the very studying of the writings of Marx himself, and of Russian writers such as Dostoevsky, is bound to create in Russia a sense of the individual as the expression of freedom.

As it has been this submerging of freedom in the objective that has enabled marxism to play such a role in the East, it was this same failing that has ultimately prevented marxism from being a dominant intellectual force in the West. Our civilization, for all its faults, has given many of its members a sense of themselves as free, a sense that their ultimate destiny was more than of this world, and so they could not be satisfied with marxism. The West had, after all, known the spiritual law of Catholicism and the freedom of the Reformation and the Enlightenment. However much this knowledge of the spirit may have faltered and betrayed itself under the new and frightening conditions of the mass age, it has been too powerful a tradition to surrender to such a limited hope as marxism. Even when thinking of the worst sides of the Western world – the invention of mass war in Christian civilization, the greed and ruthlessness of imperialist capitalism, the vulgarity and hypocrisy of the commercial society in North America – still I do not hesitate to say that the conceptions of spiritual law and freedom have some hold in our midst and give our tradition something that Asiatic marxism does not yet have.

Even when this small boast is made, we must immediately hesitate. For obviously the progressive spirit is at least as dominant in North America as in Russia. We are obviously dedicated to one God above any other, the idea of progress and man's making of it. In any advertisement, any company report, any political speech, history making and progress cry out 'Thou shalt have no other Gods before me.' In some political speeches of recent years this spirit has reached a level of high comedy. It is also true of the lower levels of power such as labour leaders, university presidents, and ministers. In the last hundred years we have so served the idea of man the maker of progress that today we live in a society that is the very incarnation of that idea. The question thoughtful people must ask themselves is whether the progressive spirit is going to hold within itself any conception of spiritual law and freedom; or whether our history-making spirit will degenerate into a rudderless desire for domination on the part of our élites, and aimless pleasure seeking among the masses. Can the achievements of the age of progress be placed at the service of a human freedom that finds itself completed and not denied by a spiritual order?

The rest of these essays will deal with this immensely difficult question. In this discussion the philosopher's relation to it must first be made plain. It is not the function of the philosopher to speak in detail about how the contradictions of the world will be overcome in the temporal process: for instance, to predict what is going to happen in North America. The function of the philosopher is rather to think how the various sides of truth that have made themselves explicit in history may be known in their unity. At the superficial level, at least, certain great ideas appear to be in contradiction. It is the philosopher's job to search for the unity behind the contradiction. I am not saying he will find any satisfactory unity; but insofar as he does, he illuminates the meaning of existence for others and thus plays a significant role in the overcoming of those contractions in the actuality.

To proceed: the truth of natural law is that man lives within an order that he did not make and to which he must subordinate his actions; the truth of the history-making spirit is that man is free to build a society that eliminates the evils of the world. Both these assertions seem true. The difficulty is to understand how they both can be thought together. Yet the necessity of thinking them together is shown in the fact that when the conclusions of either are worked out in detail, they appear wholly unacceptable.

On the one hand, does not the idea of a divine order encourage man to accept the conditions of the world rather than to improve them? Religious societies have surely accepted the fact of scarcity, have accepted that starvation is one of the vicissitudes men may be called upon to bear, have accepted that men must earn their living by the sweat of their brow. The contemplative meditating on the wonders of the divine order, isolated and protected from the floods and famines, illustrates this acceptance. It is rebellion against this that has moved men in the age of progress. Indeed, these days when the age of progress seems to have brought such chaos and confusion, there is a tendency among many of the most sensitive and intelligent to ridicule its doctrines. This has become a very fashionable occupation among intellectuals in Europe and the United States. Clever young men are always saying that it is old-fashioned to believe in progress. This ridicule is understandable from the defeated and the empirically minded, but when it comes from Christian theologians it is a dreadful perversion of the gospel. It generally indicates a vested interest in the continuance of evil. They are saying that if man can eliminate evil, then there is no need for God. Therefore we must ridicule man's powers so as to protect God. Those who say this are themselves usually comfortable and protected from life's vicissitudes. Against this, the right of man to rebel against the conditions of the world and to improve them seems indubitable.

But as soon as this is said, the necessity for limits to man's making of history must be stated with equal force. It is undeniable that the worst crimes of the twentieth century have been perpetrated in the name of progress and man's right to make history. And we must remind ourselves that North Americans have been among the perpetrators of these progressive crimes. Surely the twentieth century has presented us with one question above all: are there any limits to history-making? The question must be in any intelligent mind whether man's domination of nature can lead to the end of human life on the planet, if not in a cataclysm of bombs, perhaps by the slow perversion of the processes of life. Here, of course, the question of limit is not necessarily seen in a moral setting, because we may be concerned with simply natural consequences. The pragmatic modern man can take the wonder and mystery from this strange revolt of nature by reducing the matter to the hypothetical: 'If people think race survival desirable, they would be wise to act in certain ways.' So the mind can be freed from the idea of categorical limit, of acts we should never do under any circumstances. But the idea of categorical limit arises inescapably when we turn from the future of the race to our relations with individual persons. This is seen most clearly when we ask the questions, 'Is there anything that we should never under any circumstances do to another human being?' 'Is there a point in the degradation of a human being where we can say that so to degrade for whatever purpose is categorically wrong?' These questions have of course faced us in the work of the Nazis. The coercive experiments of researchers upon live, conscious human beings were undertaken by the doctors because they thought that their knowledge would be extended thereby. Do we think that such practices are categorically wrong? The same problem has faced us with the Communists in the purge trials where men were degraded till they were willing to confess to having done what in fact they had not done. And this example is a better one than the previous, for let us never forget that many of the Communists who so degraded their fellow men acted for the sake of that highest good, progress. It was permissible to torture this particular man because his confession would influence the masses to make easier the proper steps to progress.

This question of limit is not confined to alien lands. More and more the élites of North America seem to deny that there is any limit to what you can do to make history. Let me illustrate: at a National Electronics Conference in 1956, an engineer [Mr C.R. Shafer] was talking about what he called bio-control. He used the following words not to describe an appalling nightmare but an interesting scientific possibility. 'The ultimate achievement of bio-control may be the control of man himself. The controlled subjects would never be permitted to think as individuals. A few months after birth a surgeon would equip each child with a socket mounted under the scalp and through electrodes reaching selected areas of the brain tissue, the child's sensory perceptions and muscular activity would be either modified or completely controlled by bio-electric signals radiating from state-controlled transmitters.' The words of this engineer are extreme. This generation may not have to surrender its children to the engineers to have sockets put in their heads. But the relevant question here is, Why not? For surely we can have no hesitation in saying that as we believe men are free, if they cannot understand the true reasons for not doing something, there is nothing to restrain them from doing it. Surely the last years have taught us not to rely too much on traditions or decent feelings, certainly not our own decent feelings. This question of limit surrounds us at all points, both important and unimportant, whatever our occupation. The scientists may be singled out as an example, because on the clarity of their vision so much of what happens will depend. If we could gain knowledge by experimenting on live, conscious human beings against their will, should we do it? Should we do it if the knowledge gained added to the happiness of the greatest number?

Once the idea of limit is admitted in extreme cases, such as cruelty or torture, it cannot of course be confined simply to such cases. It must be recognized as operative throughout all our lives. The salesman or shopkeeper who objects to the ruthlessness of the Russians may be just the person who sees no limit to enslaving poor people by selling them things on the instalment plan at outrageous rates of interest, which the poor person may not even understand. The man who objects to the persecution of the Jews may make a fortune by the ownership of slum property. The very North American rulers who have most condemned the lack of restraint in the Russians have brought about the unrestrained control of the acquisitive over all aspects of our society.

But the idea of limit is unavoidably the idea of God. If we say there is something that should never be done under any circumstances, we have said that something is absolutely wrong. We have said that the history-making spirit has come upon that which it has no right to manipulate. The standard we have come upon is a reality we must accept, not a value we create. God is that which we cannot manipulate. He is the limit of our right to change the world. In the recognition of limit, the idea of law in some form must once again become real for us. The idea of God, having been discarded as impossible and immoral, comes back in the twentieth century as men recognize that if there is no theoretical limit there is no practical limit, and any action is permissible.

7

American Morality

[When planning this series, I hoped to speak about existentialism at this point. But in going along I have found there is just too much to discuss and if something has to be cut, existentialism seems the best. Nothing is, of course, a side issue to moral philosophy, but existentialism is not basic to my central discussion. My concern has been to assess the way that English-speaking North Americans generally think about moral questions. And existentialism has not yet penetrated the general consciousness. It is a French and German phenomenon. It is, indeed, true that the study of existentialism greatly illuminates what I have called historical man. For more than any other philosophy, it has stated the reasons for believing that man has no other destiny than the historical. In my opinion the best discussion of existentialism as an ethical theory is found in Simone de Beauvoir's *The Ethics of Ambiguity*. It is also true that there are many signs of an unthought existentialism appearing among North Americans. The more arty of the television dramas from New York are these days impregnated with existentialism. Existentialism is, after all, the affirmation of man's absolute freedom in an absurd universe. As young people grow up knowing their own freedom and believing the universe to be absurd, existentialism is bound to flourish. I meet it now often among the more sensitive children of prosperous parents. If our general moral tradition continues to descend into flabbiness and chaos, existentialism will extend its influence over those who wish to revolt against that chaos and yet can find no basis for hope. Nevertheless, at the moment it is not a first order problem with us in North America. Therefore I am not going to discuss it tonight.

Rather what I want to discuss is the way in which North Americans generally think and speak about moral issues. As I have said, I reject marxism, as giving an inadequate recognition of spiritual freedom and spiritual law. The question for us is whether our philosophy of progress does any better. Do we reject spiritual freedom and law more or less than marxism?

To discuss these questions it is necessary to analyse our moral language. We often take language for granted – but it is, of course, one of the subtlest and most sophisticated aspects of our humanity. A society is held together in large measure insofar as the people in it can understand a common moral language. Our actions are all the time involving other people, as their actions are involving us. And we have to communicate one with another about those actions and their purposiveness. Without some common moral language we could not so communicate.

The first thing to see about our moral language is how it has developed historically.] North American secularism has more complex roots than is often supposed. Europeans often interpret our society in a very simplified and biased manner, as if it were merely a debased edition of their own. Their indictment accuses us at one and the same time of being reactionary capitalists, and yet also of being unleavened by the ancient conservative culture. They interpret North Americans simply as materialists who had the luck to move to an uncharted continent of great resources just when European science was providing the skills to use those resources. They see us, therefore, with no moral ideas beyond the utilitarian. What they misunderstand is that the progressive secularism that holds our society is not identical with the secularism of Europe because it has in large measure arisen out of the ashes of a multiform Protestantism, particularly Puritanism. Such a predominantly Calvinist Protestantism was never long the determining force in any major European country, and Puritanism was not long dominant even in England. Whatever the influence of the vast immigration of Catholics and Jews, whatever the influence of established Catholic societies, theirs has not been the dominant tradition here. It is only necessary to understand the degree to which Jewish and Catholic institutions have had to come to terms with Protestant secularism to gauge the strength of that force. Thus at the end of the explicitly Protestant era, its spirit still implicitly forms us. To understand our modern moral language, it is necessary to see it therefore as the end product of a secularized Calvinism, or if you want it the other way, a secularism with Calvinist undertones.

It has often been considered clever to ridicule Puritanism. But those who ridiculed it have generally confused an authentic Puritanism with a hypocritical nineteenth century religion, and have not bothered to study Calvinist theology.[1] Above all it must be emphasized that Calvinism was an immensely practical faith. This is what distinguishes it from Lutheranism, which was essentially mystical. Calvin's doctrine of the Hidden God by whose inscrutable Will men were elected to salvation or damnation meant that they believed themselves cut off from the contemplation of God, except as He revealed Himself in the Bible, and particularly in Jesus Christ. Though predestinarianism and emphasis on the Fall might seem to lead to a passive quietism, they in fact led to concentration on the practical life, because men cut off from contemplation sought in practicality the assurance that they were indeed the recipients of grace. This combined with the doctrine of the priesthood of all believers led to what Max Weber has brilliantly defined as 'worldly ascetism' – the saints living practical lives in the world. Their worldly asceticism made the Calvinists an immense force in shaping history, as democratic reformers and as capitalists. Paradoxically, the rage to be confident of their election was what gave the Puritans such a sense of their own authentic freedom. Whatever may be said about the Puritan tradition, it has produced people who have known themselves as possessors of practical freedom. Also the Calvinist doctrine of the Hidden God meant that they did not believe, as have the Catholics, that one could see God's footprints in the world, and that one could discover natural law. One could only contemplate God in Jesus Christ, and go out and act as best one could. It is this tradition of acting for the best in the world that has been of such influence in creating our modern North American practicality. When freed from all theological context, it becomes pragmatism.

Because of these theological presuppositions, Calvinism was a determining force for egalitarianism. In Puritanism, more than in any other influence, lies the source of our greatest spiritual achievement in North America, social equality. It is not possible to describe here the battle over church government between Catholicism and Calvinism – the battle between the principle of hierarchy and the principle of equality. But it is clear that when you believe that every person in the Church is capable of grasping essential truth through revelation, you have a firm religious incentive towards an egalitarian rather than a hierarchical society.

I cannot here attempt to describe the long history of Protestant influence on North America or its complex interdependence with the spirit of democracy, pioneering, and science. The movement of that interdependence may be illustrated at one point only: how in educational theory the Puritans and the later immigrants have worked together to produce egalitarian technologism. This is an important example to understand because of the power of this tradition over all our educational institutions today. The immigrants who have poured into this

continent in the last hundred years have had the very understandable interest of destroying any social forms that limited
the open society. In the field of education, the decisive victory
of the technical over the older studies has allowed the open
sesame to success to consist of purely technical skill: engineering, commerce, etc. When success depends on the subtler
educational forms (the study of history and art and philosophy), it is a much more complex business for the outsider to
succeed. It was in terms of these subtler studies that most of
the immigrants had once been excluded from the privileged
classes of Europe. Inevitably therefore the ordinary immigrant
did all that was in his power to break down in education
everything but the technological.

What is interesting is the degree to which Puritan theology
encouraged this tendency. In the face of a theology of revelation, the old philosophical education, which was intended as a
means to the contemplative vision of God, became largely
beside the point. Salvation was one thing; the educational process was another. Thus they came more and more to be held
apart. The educational process gradually came to be concerned only with the teaching of techniques, so that Christians
could be effective in the world. What must be recognized is
that the democratic and secular educational system we have
today in all our schools and universities, far from being something to which Protestants have objected, is something they
have largely built themselves. There is grief and a perverse
pleasure to be derived from the irony of the fact that our present educational institutions have been created more by ministers than by any other group. This is not to say that the
ministers have always been ambitious front men pandering to
the spirit of the age. Often they did it on principle – the principle that ultimate truth had almost nothing to do with the educational process.

This formative Protestant influence has been emphasized to
show that our exaltation of the doer, the organizer, the busy

man has far deeper moral roots than a sheer surrender to materialism, as so many Europeans believe. This exaltation is the basis of our North American assumption that it is the right of the businessman to rule; to control not only our economic apparatus, but all our institutions, our politics, our churches, our schools, our universities, our newspapers, our art, and our science. Despite all that can be said against the tyranny of business, it is impossible to understand its achievements and the acceptance of its continuing power by most people unless one realizes that in and through its self-interest there has moved the idea that economic enterprise was a truly moral activity and that it served the freedom of the human spirit. How many North Americans were raised on such repressive clichés as the following from Longfellow?

> The heights by great men reached and kept
> Were not attained by sudden flight
> But they while their companions slept
> Were toiling upward in the night.[2]

How many of our Canadian bankers (of Scottish descent) still believe in such doctrine? The Alger legend of a generation ago, the outpouring of energy at home and abroad, the atmosphere of obligatory uplift among all but the highest level of businessmen cannot be interpreted solely as the hypocritical mask of exploitation. Even the glassiest financial man, whose activism has narrowed to the point of calculation, is likely to believe his activity is an instrument of progress; that he is justified to himself and to others because he has the key to the highest social good – the dynamic, expanding society. The Protestant self-made man who was the linchpin of the early industrialism has, of course, been replaced by an increasingly technical and slick set of managers among whom the old Protestant ethic has disappeared. But what remains is the belief that the activist spirit is the highest form of human life imaginable. Under early Protestantism this activism is seen as serving the Will of God;[3] in the nineteenth century the Will of God and personal gain are grossly confused, as in such men as J.P. Morgan and Rockefeller; in the twentieth century personal power combined with social engineering become ends in themselves. But always the control of the world is seen as the essentially moral.

This exaltation of activism can be seen in its negative side in the way it has inhibited those activities, such as daydreaming, sensuality, art, prayer, theoretical science, and philosophy, which do not directly change the world, and that therefore have been linked together, in contradistinction to the practical, under that exalted term, leisure. By leisure I do not mean inactivity, but those activities that are non-manipulative, which have as their ends joy rather than power, adoration rather than control. Historically, the artist, the philosopher, the mystic have been outsiders in our Protestant civilization. During the excitement over Sputnik, it was suggested that the Americans were deeply depressed by the Russian success. I thought this was a wrong interpretation. Rather, there was a great sigh of relief from the American élites, for now there was an immediate practical objective of competition to be achieved, a new frontier to be conquered – outer space. It provided further excuse not to think about what will make life meaningful when the practical problems are settled, about what people will do when the factories are filled with mechanical robots. Then, of course, leisure will have to be accepted as the most important part of life.

It is hard to catch the popular moral language in explicit form. Our very practicality has made us uninterested in systematic thought and therefore our common moral language is seldom systematized. The history-making élites of North America are not much concerned with the ideology of their power but with its exercise. Nevertheless we have a moral vocabulary that is fairly general. The remnants of a dying liberal Protestantism are combined with a potent influence from the natural sciences, and now even more from the language of the social sciences. It succeeds in exalting and uniting both capitalist enterprise and democratic equality. Of course, these influences have all shaped each other. For instance, the language of our psychology is penetrated throughout with an onward and upward optimism that it owes greatly to liberal Protestantism and which would have left a metaphysical old Jew like Freud very amused. Psychologists and YMCA secretaries now speak the same language.

It is hard to know this language for what it is, because so many of its conceptions have been de-moralized. The word 'motive' with its connotations of a free being becomes 'motivational drive' with the connotation of a robot. 'Beliefs' are now called 'attitudes,' with the implication that we have no control about what we ultimately think. Sin becomes maladjustment. The intellectual is said to intellectualize, as if thought was a front to make prejudice respectable. Conscience becomes superego, as if it were an appendage to our real selves, and so on and so on. What has happened is that psychology is thought to be a science in the narrow sense of that term. Therefore it increasingly interprets man as an object of the world. And as this psychological jargon enters our everyday speech it becomes in fact our moral language, although really it is denying that there is any such thing as morality. There is only morality if we are free. If we are beings for whom the vocabulary of attitudes, drives, and adjustment is adequate, then we are not free.

The nearest we have come to a systematic presentation of the secularized Protestant moral language is in pragmatism – the philosophy of William James and John Dewey, which was so popular in the twenties and thirties of this century. Pragmatism has had such a pervasive influence in our schools because it expressed in philosophic form much that was implicit in our way of life.

Both James and Dewey continually write about the repressive nature of traditional Protestantism and the need to free people in a scientific age from its transcendent and ironic elements. Pragmatism has therefore been interpreted as if it were a reaction against Protestantism. Indeed it is clear that Dewey and James thought it so. But this seems to me quite wrong. The whole basis of their humanism is unthinkable outside the practical Protestant ethic. Their attacks on Greek philosophy and Plato in particular have a ring completely reminiscent of the Reformers' attacks on natural theology. The Spanish-American philosopher Santayana made the very shrewd distinction between the humanisms that arise out of the Catholic tradition and those that arise in a Protestant climate. Pragmatism is the apotheosis of Protestant humanism.

What is relevant here is the pragmatists' definition of truth. Our ideas are true when and insofar as they are effective in action. To quote William James: 'The true is only the expedient in the way of our thinking, just as the right is only the expedient in the way of our acting.' Or again: 'Truth in our ideas means their power to work.' Or again: 'An idea is true as long as it is profitable in our lives.' It will be clear how far this pragmatist account of truth expresses the history-making spirit. We not only make history and nature but truth itself. To quote James again: 'Pragmatic philosophy turns towards action and power.' Contemplation, far from being an end in itself, is a dangerous pastime. To believe in the absolute, James said, was to take a moral holiday. Pragmatism is much more completely a history-making philosophy than marxism, for in Marx's philosophy man's power to make the world is limited by a final necessary outcome. In pragmatism man is entirely open to make the world as he chooses and there is no final certainty. Everything is dependent on how man uses his practical freedom. Again James' words: 'The world stands ready, malleable, waiting to receive the final touches at our hands. Like the Kingdom of Heaven it suffers human violence willingly. Man engenders truth upon it.' To digress for a moment, this sentence is an example of how our language uses Protestant metaphors with a secular meaning. The old Christian words 'final' and 'The Kingdom of Heaven' are here used in a context that utterly denies their origin. James is steeped in the old Protestant vocabulary and yet uses it to deny that there is a reality that cannot be manipulated.

What must first be mentioned about this definition of truth is its attractiveness. How appealing it is to make truth the servant of life and of our actions. The freedom of man to make the world is unambiguously asserted. The definition appears democratic and egalitarian, with its care about life, and the life of ordinary people. What gives pragmatism its power is that it catches the modern insight that the ordinary comforts of ordinary people matter in the scheme of things. The day-to-day business of living is the purpose of everything and thought is its servant. Take its educational mottoes, for instance: 'Education for Living,' 'We Learn by Doing.' Education is not being imposed on people but must serve their ordinary needs. Or as the pragmatists used to say: 'I don't teach arithmetic, I teach children.' Arithmetic becomes the servant of man; reason an instrument for fuller living. Indeed why pragmatism has been so influential with so many decent people is that it seemed such an affirmation of human freedom. It seemed a philosophy by which practical, democratic people could create a world where the full life could be lived. The exaltation of life and action above truth seemed to liberate ordinary men.

But at a deeper level, is the exaltation of life and action over truth and thought an adequate philosophic position? What does it imply in terms of spiritual law and freedom? In the last essay the possibility of law was presented in the form of the question: Is there anything that one man can do to another that is categorically wrong? Pragmatism, as the exaltation of life and action over thought, cannot give an affirmative answer to that question. If you say that the right is 'the expedient in the way of our behaving,' how can there be any room for the categorically wrong? May not the torture of children sometimes be expedient and therefore right? To say that an idea is true as long as it is profitable in our lives sounds harmless but it involves saying that the judicial condemnation of the innocent can be justified, because it is certainly often profitable in the lives of men and nations.[4] This criticism of pragmatism may be summarized in two propositions: (1) A philosophy that exalts action and life over thought cannot condemn any action as categorically wrong. (2) Any philosophy that cannot condemn certain actions as categorically wrong is in my opinion iniquitous (and I choose the adjective advisedly), whatever else it may say about anything.

To make this condemnation of pragmatism, without arguing it carefully, must not obscure how difficult it is to think the categorically wrong. We see this difficulty when we try to apply the idea of the categorically wrong to concrete cases. Is there any type of action that we can know in principle as absolutely wrong? Are there not always some circumstances that could justify a particular case? To take the example of torture: if a man had hidden a hydrogen bomb in the city of Montreal to go off at a certain hour and the police had captured him, should they torture him to persuade him to speak? Should they torture his children as a means of persuasion? Should they torture for a hydrogen bomb and not a uranium bomb, for a uranium bomb and not for TNT? Men have always found it easier to condemn torture when they were out of power than when they were responsible. The French existentialists have condemned torture by their political opponents in Algeria; they have condoned its use by their communist friends in China.

To give actuality to the idea of the categorically wrong, therefore, we must be able to state some type of action that we can know in advance that we should never do, and be able to show why such actions are inexcusable. We do not have to wait for the particular circumstances of experience in order to condemn them as wrong. Only if we can do this can we say that the idea of law makes any difference. I have borrowed the example of the judicial condemnation of the innocent because, unlike most examples, I can think of no occasions when it could be right. It can and has been argued, of course, that the judicial condemnation of the innocent is justified if it serves a wider interest, as for instance the enlightening of the masses about a conspiracy against their society. This is why certain Americans in the last years may have done it.[5] The Communist world has constantly made this its practice. It may be suggested that this type of action is wrong because it leads the law into disrespect and there is no higher interest in society than a general respect for the law; but this argument will not hold water, because if the conspiracy is carefully guarded it may not bring the law into disrespect with more than one person. If the argument then passes to the notion that the idea of the law is an image of the absolute and should never be brought into disrespect in the heart of even one person, then it implies the moral law as absolute, and depends on a justification of the wider proposition. Thus to start from assuming such a type of action is not meant as an argument for the moral law, because it obviously depends on the more general affirmation. No such wider justification is attempted in these essays. Furthermore the philosophy that would constitute such a justification is not a task of which I would be capable.[6]

What then is the value of the above condemnations of pragmatism? Its value depends on the fact that the language of pragmatism has often masqueraded as something it is not. It is therefore important to bring out its implications, namely, that it denies moral law despite all its high-sounding language. The argument has been reduced to a concrete case, in the hope that by taking theoretical assumptions to their practical limit, those assumptions may appear unacceptable. Because human beings are agents as well as intelligences, theory and practice can never be independent of each other. Theoretical propositions may lead us to reassess our practice; but equally the immediacy of practice may lead us to reassess our theories. It is therefore a legitimate argument against a theory that it leads to what may be considered morally repugnant practice. Like all forms of argument, however, it can be misused.

This argument has also been used to emphasize that men are morally responsible for what they publicly write about theory. A philosophy the principles of which can give no reason why men should not judicially condemn the innocent, indeed whose principles would seem to encourage the powerful to that condemnation, is as morally reprehensible as the actual carrying out of the deed. Recent centuries have time and again witnessed one generation laying down the theoretical basis for such iniquities and leaving it to the next generation to take the words seriously and live by them. As common sense takes practice seriously and theory cavalierly, it has been popular to condemn those who commit the iniquities, but not those who justified them. Why should this be? The language of pragmatism may seem uplifting in the mouths of James or Dewey. Obviously they and their early disciples were decent men taught by their Protestant humanism to loathe such actions as the condemnation of the innocent. Look at Dewey's actions over the Trotsky case or James's view of the Spanish-American war. Nevertheless, men are responsible for their theoretical writings. To write false theory may be more reprehensible than to organize a school badly, the bad organization of a school more harmful than the robbing of a bank. The same argument may be applied to one philosopher's justification of adultery, as compared with the simple commission of the deed. To say this is to imply nothing about the proper safeguards for freedom of opinion.

As would be expected from its Puritan origins, pragmatism has a fuller account of freedom than of law. This can be seen in relation to Dewey's influence over public education. Dewey's thought has been influential in bringing about that change in our education whereby the individual has more freedom to express his individuality, and that is surely a good. But it is equally clear that Dewey's belief that the intellect is an instrument for living has directly led to a lowering of intellectual rigour in our education. We are brought back here to the definition of the true as the expedient in our way of thinking. The Deweyite might say that it is always expedient to be able to solve some mathematical problems: so that you can excel the Russians, or because you can do more things if your mind has been trained mathematically. But why is it expedient to be able to do more things? I meet youngsters every day who can do everything they want and therefore see no purpose in a trained intellect or imagination. Indeed, there is a new type of student who is a product of the Deweyite influence on our schools. Such students have been taught by the modern world to have an unlimited sense of their own freedom but have learned in their education no intellectual interest or discipline to give content to that freedom. At the universities they are immensely aware and immensely bored. This is not meant as criticism, because their potentiality may be greater than that of those who are chugging away at success. So many professors from an entirely different era excuse themselves from coping with this boredom, by saying we have far too many poor students. They are not poor students. They are youngsters who have been taught to consider themselves free in a world where the intellect does not matter; where there is only life to be lived; there is nothing that it concerns us to know. To sum up, the pragmatists' conception of freedom ultimately fails because it does not understand the relation between freedom and thought, that is, between freedom and spiritual law.

The democratic capitalist morality cannot of course be entirely summed up in pragmatism. Nevertheless, what has been said about pragmatism indicates the direction in which our general moral language is headed. It is a language that has almost no place for the idea of spiritual law, namely, that there is a right order to our way of doing and thinking. In many ways the marxists have a greater sense of the world as a spiritual order than we do. On the other hand, we have an incomparably greater sense of the individual as the source of freedom. It is this that may yet save our democratic society from chaos. Those whose awareness of freedom becomes anguished in its alienation must seek reconciliation in an order that will not destroy their freedom but fulfil it. It cannot be known whether a sense of order will be created in sufficient people in our civilization to keep it alive, or whether the very sense of freedom will disappear first as people begin to take seriously the jargon of attitudes and adjustments.

8

Law, Freedom, and Progress

In these essays the central question of modern moral philosophy has been posed: How can we think a conception of law that does not deny the truth of our freedom or the truth of progress? This dilemma may be illustrated again because it is a dilemma of intensity and depth. The hurtling by man of objects into orbit, and indeed of himself into space is the very apotheosis of the modern spirit. Von Braun, the American rocket scientist, summed up this Faustian desire when he said, 'Man belongs to wherever he wants to go.' And already a generation ago the following words had been written on the tomb of a Russian scientist, 'Mankind will not remain bound to the earth forever.' Such words are the very affirmation of the limitless and of man's freedom as the symbol of that limitlessness. In them, modern Prometheanism affirms itself. But as I read the statement from the Russian grave, the use of the word 'bound' raises in my imagination the picture of the slavering two-headed dog the Russians have created. Men may not long remain bound to the earth, but will they remain bound by anything in what they do? As I read von Braun's statement, there comes into my mind in contrast to it, that most ironic and terrible statement of the limited: what Jesus said to Peter after the Resurrection, to comfort him for his denial. 'When thou wast young, thou girdedst thyself, and walkedst whither thou wouldest; but when thou shalt be old ... another shall gird thee, and carry thee whither thou wouldest not.'[1] By 'another' Jesus means at one level the Roman government who will have Peter crucified upside down, but also he means it will be God who will carry Peter whither he would not. Here limit is seen in all its ambiguity, for it is a law that carries evil within itself, a law that does not carry one wherever one wants to go, but whither one would not. This is the very negation of freedom and power, the acceptance of one's own death. And, what is most difficult, because this acceptance of death is in the mouth of Jesus Christ, it must be understood as an act of joy. The distance that divides the necessary from the good and that must be faced in any proper discussion of moral law is here most wonderfully expressed.

[The question is, then, how can we think an absolute morality that does not deny human freedom and the hope that evil will be overcome? And of course as I have said the idea of law involves the idea of the absolute (call it if you will the concept of God). Here, then, inevitably the discussion of moral philosophy leads to the discussion of metaphysics. What kind of a doctrine of the absolute will do proper justice to all the factors of freedom, law and progress? For instance, the most difficult question in the whole business is how one's idea of law or lawgiver, a law eternally valid and to be accepted here and now, is to be related to the idea of God, in whom all things are possible; that is, to the radical idea of God in the face of which all present structures of the world are judged inadequate. It is indeed the failure to resolve this contradiction, to see together the unchangeableness of God with the idea of a God who works in history, which finally makes me unable to accept any of the traditional theologies as adequate. It is therefore about the relation of law, freedom, and progress that I wish to speak tonight.

I must first insist I do not want to give the impression that there are neatly packaged answers to these problems. There are enough people dishing out slogans as answers to our dilemmas. In some cases they are perfectly justified in so doing. It is their business. But it is not the business of philosophy. Philosophy is destroyed when its end becomes pragmatic. We all know this kind of talk: 'Let's give our engineers a course on moral philosophy.' In saying this I am not advocating scepticism. As Kant said: 'The sceptic is the nomad of philosophy, he never settles down long enough anywhere to cultivate the soil.' No, I am not saying that philosophy has no answers. But I am saying that these true answers can only be accepted by a man as he studies the philosophers for himself. Nobody can do it for you. The study of philosophy is an end in itself.]

In approaching this problem, let me also try to make clear the point from which I think about it. For most hours of the day, human existence seems to me a crazy chaos in which I can make out no meaning and no order, a world the unspeakable evils and tragedies of which seem to have no meaning. If anyone thinks the purpose of existence is evident let him contemplate what has happened in the twentieth century; let him contemplate what is happening at the very moment that these words are read. To quote a modern saint, Simone Weil:

> To manage to love God through and beyond the misery of others is very much more difficult than to love him through and beyond one's own suffering. When one loves him through and beyond one's own suffering, this suffering is thereby transfigured; becomes, depending upon the degree of purity of that love, either expiatory or redemptive. But love is unable to transfigure the misery of others (with the exception of those who are within the range of one's influence). What saint shall transfigure the misery of the slaves who died on the cross in Rome and in the Roman provinces throughout the course of so many centuries.

To be reconciled in the face of this vision is a supernatural gift.

To those who are not so reconciled, the sense of meaninglessness should not result in a beaten retirement, but in a rage for action. If this is what the world is, let us do everything in our power to create a world where children do not starve, where men are not unemployed or burnt up by napalm. Real pessimism must surely lead to the active life and the affirmation of human freedom. It is his understanding of this that makes J.P. Sartre the clearest of modern humanists.

As soon as that sense of meaninglessness is expressed, however, I am forced to admit that I never doubt that some actions can be known to be categorically wrong. As has been repeated so often, the idea of the categorically wrong implies an order, a law, a meaning to existence. However chaotic, however crazy the world may seem, doubt is not my final standpoint, because there is that which I do not doubt. In speaking of morality, I speak ultimately from the side of the law. To do so is to affirm that the idea of God ultimately regulates moral philosophy; that the moral law is an unconditional authority of which we do not take the measure, but by which we ourselves are measured and defined; that the final judge of all moral codes is the test of the limitless, and that they can be measured first and foremost by the degree of their resistance to that test. The justification of moral law would involve showing that without such a conception, all our actions, our strivings, our decisions, our agonies must count as nothing and why they do not so count. Only a great artist could state this affirmation in the concrete; only a great philosopher could show how it can withstand any argument brought against it. As I am neither of these, it must remain in part a matter of faith for me.

Yet as soon as this is said, it must be insisted that no one should remain satisfied with the unthought content of faith that remains in any such affirmation. In this sense the philosopher must find himself as much at variance intellectually with a religion that relies solely on faith, as with a nihilistic scepticism. Religious people may say of the foregoing, 'What's all the fuss about, of course there's a moral law, now let's get on with it. After all these words, is this what philosophy leads to? There is a moral law. We knew this all the time and did not need these arguments to affirm it. We knew it on faith.' It is on these grounds that a certain kind of Protestant church-goer is always attacking philosophy. In answer, it must be emphasized that a moral code, the authority for which is based solely on faith and that makes no attempt to define itself rigorously, is a dying code, a closed morality, a morality that does not care about its own communication. It is founded on a ghetto mentality. This indeed is what certain of our Protestant churches are more and more becoming – intellectual ghettoes. In Christian terms, a morality that does not care about its own communication is condemned at its heart, because it contradicts its own first principle, charity. It is its failure in charity, just as much as its intellectual sloth, that condemns fundamentalism, in all its guises. Indeed charity and thought are here one. Those who care about charity must care about communication, and to communicate requires systematic thought. A genuine moral language must try to be universal.

This is but to return from where these essays started: the problem of a morality that can be thought stares Canadians in the face. The need for an absolute moral law is evident, just when the difficulties of thinking such a law are also most evident. It doesn't require much knowledge of Canadian society to know that the more influential people become, the less they are held by the old formulations of the moral law. It is one of the distinctive marks of North America that character and intellect are ever more in disunion. Those with character arising from faith in the traditional formulations of the law seem only to maintain that faith insofar as they are not touched by modern thought. Those who are touched by the modern world less and less maintain any sense of limit. Are the churches to say then that people are not to be educated – that the law they teach cannot withstand modern criticism? To see the problem in all its difficulty one need only ask oneself what reasons can be given in reply to a clever person who denies any categorical limits, to find that arguments turn quickly into appeals to faith. There is not space here to make the necessary distinctions for any discussion of the relation of faith to reason, but I am insisting on two points: (1) To base a moral language on an act of faith is to fail to recognize that moral language must be concerned with communication; (2) None of our traditional theologies seem to me able to provide an adequate account of what it is to think an absolute morality.[2] From this it follows that the systematic formulation of a categorical moral law is a prime necessity for Canadians. For those who can find an adequate formulation of the law in either the Catholic or Protestant theologies, this will not be a real question. Even less will it be a pressing question for those who have so entered the capitalist suburbia of the social engineers that they are happy in a relative, humanist morality.

Because the primary task of moral theory is to do the philosophy for an adequate statement of law, I wish to end these essays by raising certain theoretical issues. Otherwise it would have been tempting to end on a practical note; to write of such intricate problems as work and leisure, the proper scope of freedom and law in sexuality, the right means for the overcoming of capitalism, etc. The years since 1945 have been a time of undirected doing in which thought about practical morality has been inhibited even in those institutions, such as the universities and churches, whose special function it is. Nevertheless I will end with theoretical questions, not in any hope of dishing out slogans to our dilemmas, but to indicate the difficulties in a statement of the law. Theory always seems so unspecific to those who do not realize its constitutive power. But to be a philosopher is to know its power. Only those will be interested in philosophy who realize that as we sow in theory so will we reap in action.

The first consideration is how the moral law can be formulated in a way that does not override but fully recognizes the freedom of the spirit. The breakdown of the old systems of moral law were chiefly due to the failure of their formulations at this point. The demand of the law seemed external to the human will from which it was demanded. As men became conscious of themselves as free they believed their freedom to lie in the rejection of what was external to them. It was this recognition and rejection that is the common ground between the reformed theologians and the philosophers of the Enlightenment. Kant puts this in the fullest light of argument in his wonderful little book *The Groundwork of the Metaphysics of Morals*. He says there that if the law is to be moral it must be a law that is freely obeyed. It is not a moral act to obey the law, except in freedom. Thereby good acts are distinguished from right acts and it is shown that morality is first and foremost concerned with right acts. This being so, the moral law depends upon our freedom. To use Kant's metaphor, in morality men self-legislate the law. Yet the question immediately arises how this spirit of independence proper to morality can be reconciled with the spirit of dependence proper to adoration. It is around the discussion of freedom and law, therefore, that what was put simply in an earlier essay about being one's own or not one's own can be properly thought.

Practically, the clear recognition of this problem is of especial consequence in our society, where our long tradition of Protestantism has taught men to know themselves as free in a very direct way. Indeed there are still some people in our society who can accept the law as something given, rather than as something self-legislated. But such a morality of authority will have less and less significance in our society, particularly as the conditions of our lives are more and more rationalized in a scientific era. To rely on an external morality in such a period of history produces people who revolt from the conception of moral law itself.

This was illustrated recently when incidents with drugs occurred among teen-agers in Halifax. The reaction of many older people to this evidence was simply to advocate all kinds of external methods to keep the young within the limits of the traditional morality. It was significant that this appeal to external law came particularly from Protestants, who seem to have forgotten that the origin of Protestantism lay in an affirmation of the primacy of the Gospel over the law. This is but an illustration of how emptied Protestantism has been of its original magnificent affirmations. Of course some external precautions have to be taken. One obviously must try to prevent by police action criminals selling drugs to the young. But such external methods are only palliatives and have little to do with the far more important question of how young people are to become self-legislating. A law that incipient adults can accept must be a law that has meaning for them and springs from their own freedom. Therefore, the methods for producing that self-knowledge cannot be external but must go to the very roots of the educational process. Technological education plus pious pep talks are not enough. This is more than simply a question of educational means, because the right educational means can only arise among people who are thinking carefully about the proper theoretical relation between freedom and law.

[In asserting the principle that the formulation of the moral law must include within itself an adequate account of human freedom, I recognize how dangerously the principle may be abused. The abuse is to say that the moral law must suit every whim. I think this abuse is illustrated every time one reads *Maclean's* magazine. There are more and more articles in *Maclean's* about moral questions and these articles are written from the standpoint of attacking the old moral laws in the name of what suits Toronto suburbia and popular psychology. And I must admit that when I read this stuff in *Maclean's* my first reaction is always a strict moral conservatism. Let's just exalt some objective moral code clearly defined against this soft and vacuous nonsense, (an exercise) which makes the moral law a tame confederate of the Toronto Granite Club. But nevertheless I am wrong in my reaction. However foolish these *Maclean's* articles may be in detail they proceed from a correct principle, that the limits men impose upon themselves in an age of reason must be self-imposed and must arise as the fulfilment, not the denial, of human freedom.]

Yet the difficulty of the problem is also illustrated from the fact that in the practical world there is a continual danger in making the law dependent on our freedom. The abuse is to write as if the moral law must pander to every whim. This abuse is well illustrated by the articles about moral questions that appear in our mass circulation magazines – articles about the marriage bed, divorce, education, etc. These articles are written for middle-class consumption and therefore interpret the moral law to suit the convenience of suburbia and the supposed facts of popular psychology. They illustrate how easily the principle of the dependence of the law upon freedom can reduce the moral law to a tame confederate of the Lares and Penates of the country club. It was the application of this same principle in the immanentisms of the nineteenth century that gradually eliminated from them any idea of limit.

These practical dangers lead obviously to the dilemmas of theory. Yet it must be insisted how complicated it is to achieve theoretical clarity at this point. To illustrate: the Kantian conception of freedom cannot be reconciled with the old conception of substance, on which the philosophies of natural law were based. It is this that Hegel is insisting on in his preface to *The Phenomenology of Mind* when he says that the ultimate meaning of the modern spirit is to think the absolute as subject, not as simple substance. But it is the ancient philosophy of substance that allowed men to use such a word as 'soul.' The problem then arises how we can think any doctrine of

personality if we cannot think of the soul as substance. Indeed
the claim is made by the philosophers of the ancient persuasion that it is just this giving up of the doctrine of substance
that has meant that modern philosophy can have no doctrine
of limit and therefore can show no resistance to the test of the
limitless. To illustrate the complexity again: does not the metaphor of a self-legislated moral law stem from and result in the
doctrine of many mystics that man is necessary to God? Clearly
such a doctrine cannot be reconciled with the traditional conception of creation. But does not the idea that we must be limited in our conduct depend on the doctrine that we are created?

These metaphysical issues have been raised to show what
deep waters surround the question of law and freedom; to
show that a reformulation of the moral law cannot be made
without the closest scholarship. Above all it is necessary to
think about these problems in the light of the history of philosophy. And in that history what is most important is to grasp
the differing imports of ancient and modern thought. One of
the tragedies of the modern society is that those of the ancient
persuasion have a rich and comprehensive knowledge of
Greek philosophy and the Christian commentary thereon,
while often lacking any close knowledge of the moderns; on
the other hand, those who see the modern problems often have
only scanty knowledge of the relevance of ancient philosophy.
It must be insisted that the true relation of freedom to law can
only be thought by those who have immersed themselves in
the history of philosophy.

A second theoretical issue is how the doctrine of law can
be properly related to a doctrine of history that includes what
is true about progress. It is necessary to bring into unity the
idea of the unchangingness of God with the idea of God who
works in history. The idea of a law eternally valid and to be
accepted here and now must be related to the idea of God in
whom all things are possible; that is, to the idea of God before
whom all the present structures of the world are to be judged

inadequate. To put the metaphysical problem in its moral and political setting: all progressive moralities are condemned as not being able to withstand the temptation of the limitless. There is no place in their theory for saying 'no' to certain types of action. Because there is no place for the categorical 'no,' they cannot understand the absoluteness of sin. It is this superficiality about sin that above all leads so many disciples of progress to indulge or acquiesce in appalling means. Yet the doctrine of limit can so easily be used to make sacrosanct the particular structures of the present – whether in economics, politics or metaphysics – and by so doing to eliminate from our minds the hope and the determination that the evils of this world will yet be overcome. As against the unthought progressivism of modern society that seems to move towards the future with no sense of purpose, it is no wonder that conservatism has become popular among thinking people in the western world. The truth of conservatism is the truth of order and limit, both in social and personal life. But obviously conservatism by itself will not do. For it can say nothing about the overcoming of evil, and at its worst implies that certain evils are a continuing necessity. Let us admit how terribly the powers of this world have used the phrase 'the poor we have always with us.' Against this the truth of radicalism is just the unlimited hope that evil is not necessary. This is why the great Utopian thinkers have developed when a religious, political, and economic structure is being deified. In our modern world the greatest of these Utopian prophets was Marx. As against the capitalist order that made absolute such concepts as the law of supply and demand, and particular property relations, that in fact meant acceptance of the evils that went with them, Marx held up a total denial of the world as it was in the name of the ecstatic hope that in history all things are possible, and evil never necessary. [Speaking in Canadian political terms, we certainly have need of order and of limit, but it must not be a law that in effect simply deifies our present system of property relation and the control of the greedy over our nation. We have had just such an economic policy in Canada in our age of expansion since 1945.]

To put the problem directly in terms of our contemporary society: there can be no doubt that we all have need of a proper conservatism, an order that gives form to persons, to families, to education, to worship, to politics, and to the economic system. Yet to express conservatism in Canada means de facto to justify the continuing rule of the businessman and the right of the greedy to turn all activities into sources of personal gain. The conservative idea of law has often been in the mouths of the capitalists, but seldom in their actions. Their economic policy has been the denial of order and form. It has been carried out by exalting the impulse that is the very symbol of the unlimited and the disordered. As a ruling class they stand condemned for their denial of law. Thus it is almost impossible to express the truth of conservatism in our society without seeming to justify our present capitalism. To avoid this, a careful theory is needed in which the idea of limit includes within itself a doctrine of history as the sphere for the overcoming of evil.

These dilemmas of moral and political theory are dependent on the metaphysical dilemmas that surround the doctrine of God. The doctrine of God must allow the cry '*Veni Creator Spiritus*' as the affirmation that all the present structures of the world will yet be superseded; but it must also allow the imposition of structure on our selves and society in the here and now. On the one hand, such a reconciliation does not seem possible within the division between natural and revealed religion, which underlay the old metaphysics. On the other hand, it does not seem possible within modern immanentism, which tends to eliminate the idea of eternity from the idea of God, and which either degenerates into undefined liberal platitudes or reacts into a biblicism that denies philosophy. Even to approach this problem requires the analysis of a complex of metaphysical questions. Our doctrine of God will only become more adequate if a multitude of philosophers give their time to rethinking in the greatest detail such concepts as 'purpose,' 'revelation,' 'progress,' 'time,' 'history,' 'nature,' and above all, 'freedom' and 'evil.'

From this complex of metaphysical questions about God, one stands out as being of particular significance and difficulty: the true conception of nature and its relation to history. As I have said, history has been understood by modern men as the imposition of their freedom upon nature. This has led to a view of nature as infinitely malleable. Nature has meaning only in relation to ourselves. The extremity of this view not only raises the question of the limits of our manipulation, but also the fact that within such a view there can be no natural joy for us. Art and love can only find their fulfilment in a vision of nature in opposition to our freedom. For instance, it is surely the spirit of domination that has frustrated a proper respect for sexuality on this continent, even if that frustration takes the outward form of a too great engrossment with it. Indeed we may say that the spirit knowing itself as free cannot rest in natural joy. Nevertheless it cannot deny natural joy without paying the terrible price of those fantastic revolts of a perverted nature that have so characterized the twentieth century.

What doctrine of nature will be adequate to express [the idea] that nature is a sphere for our timeless enjoyment and yet also a sphere that we must organize, that it has meaning apart from our ends and yet is also part of redemptive history? Obviously the Aristotelian conception of nature can no longer hold us, as we have passed beyond it in the science of the last centuries. A philosophic reconstruction of the concept of nature is necessary, but of consummate difficulty, because it must take into itself what the modern scientists have discovered. The hope that there will be such a reconstruction is strengthened when one sees the speculations of some few theoretical scientists, mainly in Europe. Take such a book as *The*

History of Nature by the German physicist von Weiszäcker. Von Weiszäcker's view of nature quite transcends that of something to be dominated. He has after all lived through the twentieth century in Germany. Yet he does not exclude history from nature. He does not see nature as some timeless entity outside the historical process. He seems to be moving to a doctrine of nature that overcomes the distinction between practical and theoretical science, that overcomes the distinction between nature as the simply dominated and nature as the simply contemplated.

The theoretical dissatisfaction of von Weiszäcker is not often to be met with among scientists. Yet with such people does our hope lie. Insofar as artists come to take their art seriously and try to think and practise it within a fuller perspective; insofar as scientists think the meaning of their own work in relation to being as well as to history; insofar as practical men of all sorts and conditions think deeply about what they are doing; and insofar as meta-physicians, in fear and trembling are not content with inadequate unities, the contradictions of our present practice may yet be overcome. A morality that does not scorn joy and relates it to suffering may perhaps arise. Whether or how this will happen in our particular civilization cannot be determined. What can be determined however, within this present, is enough to enable us to at least try, with the very Word Himself, to take the cup and give thanks.

Dr Grant Answers Questions Raised in Letters from Listeners

I would like to say thank you to all of the people who sent me letters, and particularly to those who included questions about philosophy, or wrote down why they disagreed with various things I'd said.

Tonight I intend to say what I think about certain of the questions asked, particularly when the same kind of question was asked by various people. There are three types of letters, however, that I won't be able to answer. The first type is from those who posed their question basically as an accusation of bad faith. For instance, the kind of question that says 'Don't you really believe in an absolute moral law because you don't enjoy life or because you are a reactionary, etc?' One letter accused me of a particular form of activity that I had never heard of and that sent me hotfoot to my Krafft-Ebing. Now, I cannot answer these letters because they are not to do with philosophy, not because of any claim to good faith. One of the most deadly things about our society is the claim that we are all really wanting the best, when in fact we are all moved by most devious motives. I'm sure I am as filled with them as anybody. But still such questions aren't philosophy. I say this because these letters represent a tendency in modern thought –

to interpret the truth or falsity of something in terms of psychological causes. For instance, there has been a recent book in England interpreting the philosophy of Berkeley as arising from the fact that Berkeley was fixated at the anal stage of his childhood development. Now this kind of talk is interesting and it is useful for all of us to think about it in connection with ourselves, but my objection to it is when it is used to bypass the question 'what is true and what is false?' in philosophy, and these psychological explanations are often used for just this purpose. The question that interests me about Bishop Berkeley is whether what he said about our perceptions is a true account of perceiving. And the training his parents gave him on the pot seems to be not of determining significance.

The second type I cannot answer is the kind of question that is of such excellence and of such profundity that I could only discuss it in detail with the person who sent it. A listener in Victoria, for instance, has written down some brilliant and subtle questions about what we mean by causality. He is obviously a person who has thought deeply about philosophy for many more years than I and it would be impertinent on my part to answer in short space what I think of causality when applied to morality and history. I have received various letters of this sort dealing with very intricate metaphysical questions. I hope to be able to answer them directly by mail when I have clarified my mind on the issues concerned. These are all issues where very sharp distinctions must be made, and very careful vocabulary employed.

The third type I cannot answer includes what I would call the really wild letters, and I don't mean the term 'wild' in any sense of the term of abuse. For anybody who gives himself to life at all must be full of wildness and craziness. The people the world calls sane are often those who have just closed themselves off from life. Do you remember what Dr Johnson said to his cautious friends about Kit Smart? But these letters are too individual to speak about in a public broadcast. I really go for these crazy letters – what I call Kerouac–Dean Moriarty letters. One thing that is interesting is how many of these letters come from Vancouver. What a relief they are to somebody who spends the winter in cautious old Halifax. Do you remember Hegel's wonderful metaphor about the process through which philosophical truth is established – the bacchanalian revel where not a soul is sober?

Now to say something about those questions that have been asked most often. Many people asked what I meant by archetype. I think the question that was asked could best be put in this way: 'In what way, if at all, do we still partake of archetypes, as the men of the primitive culture?' My answer would be this: We still, of course, partake of archetypes in religious rituals. And in so far as we share in any ritual, however far removed from explicit religion, we do still experience to some small extent life in the archaic way. This undoubtedly becomes more and more rare in conditions of urban industrial life, where the pressure of the historic sense is so great. Of course, outside the Christian liturgy, the archetypes that give significance to our actions are not sacred in the sense of the supernatural as they were to archaic man, but only sacred in the sense that tradition can make them so. Insofar as any of us do still experience in the ancient way, it is mainly in relation to our sense of time.

Of course we may be conscious of time in the two different ways at once: that is, both in the archaic and modern sense of time. We may live through such events as marriage, birth, death, and burial (that is the death and burial of those we love) as overwhelmingly new and unique in their personal context, yet at the same time be aware of them as ancient, archetypal, impersonal, heavy with the weight of the sacred. Whenever we look back to some pattern in the past, to a perfection already achieved, and never again to be reached but only imitated, then we are in some sense thinking as did archaic man. We do this in varying degrees, in many contexts, more or less trivial. When we celebrate traditional feasts with secular rituals, as at Christmas, Easter, Halloween – even in our welcoming of the seasons, finding the first mayflower, etc. – actions that are significant not because they are new and ours, but because they are repetitive, ancient, universal. Even food may take on a sacred quality. The pie that mother used to bake was in some sense laid up in heaven, in contrast to every cake mix that is labelled new. The advertisers in the commercial world are, of course, aware of the power of the archetypes and use them. Still more often they use the historic sense of time. This toothpaste is unique because it alone has this new chemical in it. But Mother's Day, for instance, is a good example of commercial exploitation of one of our most archetypally sacred conceptions. I would say also that women, more usually, can continue to inhabit this archetypal world than men. And that is why when a society is breaking up women often maintain a greater health than men. Of course, what is also true is when women are broken they seem capable of even greater [moral and spiritual] perversions than men.

Another question a lot of people asked was why I asserted so categorically that I believed there was an overall meaning to history – why I believed history to be no arbitrary or exponential process. Various people wrote to say that, 'if you attempt to see meaning in history aren't you forcing all the manifold events of history into a strait-jacket, which only expresses one person's interpretation of the matter? Isn't it true that the more knowledge we have of historical facts the less we can see any pattern or point in them? Isn't Toynbee just the perfect example of a man who tries to force all the facts of history into particular patterns and he becomes dishonest in doing so?' Now in answering this question I would make a distinction here between the historian and the philosopher. I agree that when one is an historian who observes history and whose business it is to recount honestly and in the light of a careful examination of the evidence what has been going on in human existence, there is no need to state that there is an overall pattern as to what has been going on. That is, qua historian, the individual need find no meaning arising from the facts he studies. I think one can be a perfectly good scientific historian and see no meaning to history.

But when a man becomes a philosopher he is in a different relation to these facts; for a philosopher is not only viewing the facts from the position of observer, he knows that he is a person who is seeking to understand the meaning of his own life. And I must point out that the most unimportant events of our own lives are as much historical events as the Battle of Waterloo or the Peace of Westphalia. Then the question is: Is there any meaning to the events of my life? And if one answers that affirmatively, one must move from the meaning of one's own life to the meaning of all lives. And one comes to recognize that if there is meaning to certain events there must be meaning to all events. And that is to say that there is meaning to history. But what I am saying is that one's answer to the question, 'Is there meaning in history?,' is not something that arises first from studying history, but something that arises from the study of philosophy, and that philosophy brings to history. And let us never forget that philosophy stands or falls by its ability to transcend history.

Now it is at this level that I would criticize Toynbee. I do not criticize Toynbee because he says there is meaning to history, but because he says our knowledge of that meaning arises directly from the scientific study of history. Of course it doesn't. And this can be seen from the fact that perfectly honest scientific historians can differ about the question whether there is meaning in history. That is, when I made the statement that history is no arbitrary or accidental process I was not making an historical statement, but a philosophic one. It would be to pass beyond this to say what I think the meaning of history is, for instance, to discuss the question of what truth and what inadequacy there is in the idea of progress. To do that I would have to write down a detailed and careful philosophy of history. But where the people who asked this question seemed to me to have been quite right, is that throughout all my talks I have been assuming a philosophy of history, which is, in my opinion, true. I do not think it is possible to speak about the questions of moral philosophy outside the question of what is history.

Another question. A lot of people asked me what I thought of the society of the Soviet Union in the light of what I had said about Marx as a great prophet. There seem to me [to be] two distinct questions involved here. First, what is good and what is bad in modern Soviet society? Second, how much marxian prophecy is responsible for what is good and what is bad in the Soviet Union? These are distinct questions, and they are distinct questions, again, for two reasons. First, marxism did not come into a vacuum in Russia. There was a long history in Russia before 1917. And much that is bad in Russia and much that is good may owe its roots to that history which is quite apart from marxism. And secondly, marxism was brought to Russia by people who interpreted Marx in a particular way. I think, of course, especially of Lenin. Therefore someone might say that some of the worst things in the Soviet Union arise from a perverted marxism and not a true marxism. Obviously, before we can judge what is good and bad in the Soviet Union, we must first study what is going on in that society. The study of what is going on in another civilization is, of course, a science of great subtlety. And we rely on the finding of sciences in such studies, or at least we should rely on them and not on propaganda, whether pro or contra.

As in all spheres there will be good and bad scientists. And here indeed is a sphere in which dishonesty is well paid. And it will be the duty of any student of Soviet civilization to determine the influence of marxism in that society. But what the philosopher can determine is the adequacy of marxism as an account of human existence. Here I need only repeat what I have said earlier: marxism has extremely brilliant insights into the course of modern civilization. Also, where existentialism is the most lucid of modern humanisms, marxism seems to me the noblest. Yet for all this, it does not seem to me to give an adequate account of freedom or moral law.

One caution I would, however, like to make. Nothing has done and will do more harm in the course of our own society than to keep our attention too fixed on Soviet society. It turns us away from correct judgment as to what should happen here. During the last decade, for instance, so much time was spent by educated men speaking of our first task being the maintenance of the free world against communist tyranny. At the same time, the Howes and the Taylors were subordinating all ends of our society to the interest of big business. As I have said, all our institutions, particularly those of the mind, were being shaped in the image of state capitalists, so that the language the diplomats used about free society sounded hollower and hollower. Our first social concern must be qualitative judgment about our own, and we can be distracted from these by any fixation with Russia.

By far the most letters I have received have concerned the conception of law and the idea of the absolutely right and wrong. These took many forms: defences of pragmatism, assertions that an absolute morality was antique in a scientific age, statements that I pulled limits out of a hat without rational justification. There was, however, a consistent position that gives unity to many of these letters. I would therefore like to state that position and comment on it. The position I am going to describe is against what I have said about the idea of the absolutely wrong being necessary to thought. I singled out pragmatism for condemnation along these lines because of its influence in North America. But of course what I have said applies equally to any naturalistic philosophy – for instance, those ethical systems that find their prime inspiration in the truth of evolution, or any other scientific proof.

Now the central criticism of what I have said has been the following – I hope I put it fairly. 'Isn't it in fact just those people
who believe in moral absolutes who have practised the very
ruthlessness to which you object? Aren't the worst cases of
persecution in history associated with absolutist fanatics?'
Several people writing mentioned the Inquisition in Spain, the
purge trials in Russia, and implied that it was on absolutist
grounds that the late Senator McCarthy perpetrated his worst
iniquities. Therefore, isn't it true to say that scepticism is the
foundation of tolerance and that only as we know that we can
be certain of nothing do we come to take that proper respect
for other people? That is, after all, the foundation of any true
morality. Aren't the sceptics the people who are truly tolerant
and moderate and aware of limits? Some people who argued
this way went on to say that it does no harm to say that moral
standards are relative or a matter of convenience. What does
matter is that people who don't like torture, who don't like the
judicial condemnation of the innocent, should influence society to produce in other people the same feeling. Now, I would
like first to say what seems to me of substance in this position.
First, I think scepticism is a necessary method for any educated man, and this includes scepticism about our own deepest
opinions so that we don't get a vested interest in certain opinions and hold them as idols. It is this indeed that makes philosophy necessary in a civilized community; the critical and
sceptical side of philosophy is necessary if we are to escape
idolatry. St Augustine once spoke of philosophy as being *ex
umbris et imaginibus in veritatem*, that is, 'out of the shadows
and the imaginings, into the truth.' And of course scepticism
is necessary if we are not to confuse the shadows and the
imaginings with the truth. But I don't think this scepticism
should include doubting that there is truth that will make us
free. Oliver Cromwell once said to some fanatics of his day, 'I
beseech you by the bowels of Christ that you may consider the
possibility that you are mistaken.' I think we should all be con-

stantly considering the possibility that we are mistaken about this or that. I believe that this kind of consideration will make us more tolerant.

Secondly, I would also agree as a fact that some of the most terrible crimes of history, against love and decency, have been committed by those who believe in absolutes and this is a fact of history it behooves us to remember. The persecutions that have been carried out in the name of Jesus seem more repugnant than those crimes that have been done in the name of greed or power – even if they have been justified before the court of social order.

I would also like to bring out the point, which I did not make sufficiently clearly before, that I recognize that the issue of the categorically wrong only becomes difficult when we bring it down to concrete cases. Can you ever say about any type of action that you can know in advance that it can never be done under any circumstance? Aren't there always particular circumstances that justify certain types of action? For instance, [as I have said before,] let's say a man has hidden a hydrogen bomb somewhere in the city of Montreal to go off at a certain hour. The police capture him. Shouldn't they torture him to find out where the bomb is? The point that I am trying to make is that the idea of moral law is no good unless there are certain actions that can be known in advance as categorically wrong, and isn't this what we just cannot know. It was for this reason that I borrowed, and with great care, the example of the judicial condemnation of the innocent, because it seems to me a crystal-clear case of what I mean. This is something we can know in advance we should never do. This is something we do not have to wait for the particular circumstances of experience to decide whether it is right or wrong. What I have maintained is that this is something we can know is out of the question before the case arises. We have here a type of action that implies the law and about which we can speak universally.

Now a student said to me about this type of action, 'Couldn't you justify it if by condemning a man who is innocent of a particular crime you brought home to society as a whole the danger of the communist conspiracy?' Now this is what the Americans in the last years have either done or come very close to doing. The evidence about the Hiss and Remington cases is not yet absolutely clear. And of course, the Russians have done it. Isn't it because Nixon seems to have come close to this kind of thing that one is terrified of him becoming President of the United States? However arrogant, however foolish, however twisted Hiss may have been, if you say that if he was innocent of the crime for which he was being tried he should not have been condemned, and if you say this is not just your feeling but is a principle, then you are saying what I am trying to say. Now as I have admitted, I cannot see yet with absolute clarity how this principle can be said to be true. But I find it absolutely impossible to think its denial. Do we ever come nearer to what convinces us than this?

Now pragmatism by its very definition cannot say anything in advance about such questions. It in fact denies that we can ever say anything about moral law in advance and therefore denies the concept of moral law itself. Now I want to make absolutely clear that I am not judging pragmatism on its consequences in the world – to do so would be to fall into the pragmatic way of thinking. That is to substitute one pragmatism for another; pragmatists judge actions by their consequences. Of one thing I am sure, the defence of a moral law cannot rest itself on an appeal to consequences.

In practice, what I am saying is that the judicial condemnation of the innocent is not said to be wrong because of its consequences. It is to be judged wrong irrespective of its consequences. This is what I meant by law. There must be a law by which we judge consequences and which is thought to be quite apart from experience. The finite is judged by the infinite and not vice versa.

One thing that confuses this issue greatly is that the truth of this is confused with the truth of its relation to other questions of grave difficulty, questions that come from political philosophy, two in particular – first, the authority of particular institutions to state what the moral law is in particular cases, and second, the use of force by these institutions or through them by the state to make people conform to these particular cases. To speak clearly about either of these questions very careful distinctions will have to be made. It is with these kind of distinctions that the body of political theory is concerned. Let us face it, for an individual to live an educated moral life he must learn to make these careful distinctions. I would say, for instance, that people who have believed in absolutes and who have persecuted throughout history have failed at this point, not over the question of the ultimate truth of an absolutist moral theory. But they have failed to make the distinction between the absolute and the particular institutions of history. They have failed to make the proper distinction between love and freedom and law. It is on these grounds that we may fairly say that they were wrong – not on the grounds that they asserted a moral law.

On the other hand, I suggest that the pragmatists are wrong in denying moral law because in so doing they are denying not only the interpretations of moral questions, but they are also denying the very idea of morality itself. They have therefore no right to masquerade as moral philosophers because they are denying that which they are philosophizing about. Now of course [other] people can take the argument from here because what I have said is only a prolegomena to the question.

The last question I would like to speak about was asked by many people. What they said was this: 'What you have spoken about concerns the history of thought, but how does all this academic stuff help me to decide moral problems here and now?' I would like to say first that I hardly see it as my function to stand up before a microphone and to exhort everybody to be moral, or even to discuss the pros and cons of bilking the income tax. Such persuasion of people to do good actions is the role of the preacher, and a very important role it is. But it is not the role of the philosopher. What I have tried to do in this introduction is to illuminate some of the assumptions and implications involved in our modern moral thinking and speaking, partly by seeing them within their historical context. This is one way by which our self-consciousness may be gradually increased. Insofar as understanding increases our self-consciousness, it increases at the same time our freedom, and thereby our openness both to moral and to immoral actions. I've tried to emphasize that we live in the age of reason with all the terrible capacity for good and evil that that involves. In such an age, we more then ever need the rational freedom of self-knowledge with which to legislate our own laws and limits. Let me take but one example, chastity, and by chastity I do not in any sense mean a refusal of sexuality, but the giving of sexuality its proper place in a whole human existence. Until recently, the ordering of sexuality in our lives was enforced not only by principles but by fear of results, in other words by expediency. Soon science will have perfected devices for the avoidance of results. In so doing the problem will have moved more out of the realm of expediency into the realm of morality, pure and simple. The need to know what we are doing and why is too obvious to need much stressing. In such an age, philosophic thought presents itself to us in all its immediacy. How can we know the purpose and point of our existence? Of course, I do not mean thereby to say that philosophy is simply the servant of the practical. Moral philosophy is by definition concerned with the practical. But in solving practical problems it points beyond itself to the act of knowing, which is its own reward. It is better to arrive than to journey.

APPENDIX 2

Introduction to the 1966 Edition

This book was written seven years ago and since that time I have changed my mind about certain questions in moral philosophy. It is not surprising that this should happen. Moral philosophy attempts to answer the question, 'What constitutes the good life?,' and is therefore a science in which it is difficult to achieve clarity. Life would be an empty affair indeed, if we did not see this question in a deepening way as we mature.

Ours is a period of history in which clarity about the problems of moral philosophy is particularly difficult. The chief reason for this difficulty is the dominance of technique over all aspects of our lives. I consider technique to be, 'the totality of methods rationally arrived at and having absolute efficiency (for a given stage of development) in every field of human activity.'[1] In the last several centuries most human beings have come to believe with growing certainty that all human problems can be settled by technical skill. This belief has made technique their morality and today it can be truly said that the only living morality of our society is faith in technique. This fact is often hidden by the popular liberal platitude, 'We can use technology for good or evil according to the values we choose.' We should not, however, be deluded by this platitude into thinking that technique is any longer the servant of mankind. The pursuit of technological advance is what constitutes human excellence in our age and therefore it is our morality. Negatively, faith in technique only achieved this supreme status as its worshippers (often philosophers) ridiculed all the moral traditions of the past that doubted the dogma that human beings could solve all their problems by technique.

In the situation where technique is victorious the individual finds himself in a new relation to tradition. The tradition that he inherits is at once more monolithic than any previous one and, at the same time, by its very nature is hostile to the moral teachings of the past. We live in a society where more men worship the same god than ever before, but the cult of that god can find no easily fixed forms. In North America the theology of technique goes by the name of liberalism. I mean by liberalism the belief that man's essence is his freedom. Our society functions effectively because liberalism is the doctrine that best expresses the needs of technology – far better than its chief public rival in the East. Society would not work so well if its dominant classes were not committed to that creed, and if the masses did not give it at least passive allegiance. Most individuals must live within the dominant morality of their age. They do not need moral philosophy; they need liberal sermons, and, if they become more sophisticated, the systematic exposition of progressive dogma. There is plenty of both abroad, for it is always easy to find flatterers of the spirit of the age.

Men being what they are, however, there are some who cannot find an adequate moral philosophy in the self-authenticating worship of technique and the liberalism that rationalizes it. If a man still hungers for the bread of eternal life in the midst of the modern dynamism, he must seek to satisfy that hunger, even though he knows his talents are limited. Since the modern age has destroyed as living options all other traditions but itself, such people must turn back to the past in the hope of finding there what has been lost in the dynamic present. As the past has been demolished as a living continuity, men can no longer inherit it in their day-to-day lives; they must set themselves the task of being miners of the buried past. The serious entry into the human past is a prodigious event in the life of any individual. By 'serious' I mean an entry into the past not simply as an antiquarian interest (such as the false mandarinism that characterizes much university scholarship) but as a search for good that can be appropriated to the present. Such an entry is a prodigious event because the individual who makes it is faced with charting the subtle and diverse elements that compose the moral philosophy of the era. It is the difficulty of this charting that makes the writing of moral philosophy such a perilous task in our age.

Philosophy in the Mass Age was an attempt to put down in popular form some observations about the moral traditions of the West. When I wrote it, my mind was deeply divided about the relation between those traditions and the religion of progress. Some glimmering of what it was to believe in an eternal order had been vouchsafed to me so that I was no longer totally held by the liberal faith. I believed in a moral order that men did not measure and define but by which we were measured and defined. At the practical level, I had seen many of the limitations of the technological society. Nevertheless, I was still held by the progressive dogma. It is hard indeed to overrate the importance of faith in progress through technology to those brought up in the main stream of North American life. It is the very ground of their being. The loss of this faith for a North American is equivalent to the loss of himself and the knowledge of how to live. The ferocious events of the twentieth century may batter the outposts of that faith, dim intuitions of the eternal order may put some of its consequences into question, but its central core is not easily surrendered. Its bastion is the trust in that science that issues in the

conquest of nature, human and non-human. Every moment of
our existence is so surrounded by the benefits of technology
that to try to understand the limits to its conquests, and also its
relation to human excellence, may seem the work of a neurotic seeking to escape from life into dreams.

Philosophy in the Mass Age expresses clearly that uncertainty in my mind about the progressive faith. The basic presuppositions of that faith are still present in it, even when
some of the dogma's formulations are shown to tend towards
immoral practice. The book is therefore permeated with the
faith that human history for all its pain and ambiguities is
somehow to be seen as the progressive incarnation of reason.
What had been lost in the immediacy of the North American
technological drive would be regained, and regained at a higher level because of the leisure made possible by technology. It
might seem that we were losing the idea that morality had any
eternal reference, that we were entering a society where anything goes; it might be that contemplation of final cause was
disappearing from the multiversities that served our system; it
might be that art had lost all reference beyond the subjective
and the entertaining. While all of this seemed to be true, it was
balanced by the belief that all that was lost would soon be
regained. When technology had reached a certain stage it
would once again serve human purposes. Thus, our society
would have within itself all that was good in the antique world
and yet keep all the benefits of technology.

At the theoretical level, I considered Hegel the greatest of
all philosophers. He had partaken of all that was true and
beautiful and good in the Greek world and was able to synthe-
size it with Christianity and with the freedom of the enlightenment and modern science. It cannot be insisted too often how
hard it is for anyone who believes the Western Christian doctrine of providence to avoid reaching the conclusion that
Hegel has understood the implications of that doctrine better
than any other thinker. I therefore attempted to write down in

non-professional language the substance of the vision that the age of reason was beginning to dawn and [dawn] first in North America.

Since that day my mind has changed. In the practical realm, I am much less optimistic about the effects that a society dominated by technology has on the individuals that comprise it. I no longer believe that technology is simply a matter of means, which men can use well or badly. As an end in itself, it inhibits the pursuit of other ends in the society it controls. Thus, its effect is debasing our conceptions of human excellence. So pervasive and deep-rooted is the faith that all human problems will be solved by unlimited technological development that it is a terrible moment for the individual when he crosses the Rubicon and puts that faith into question. To do so implies that unlimited technological development presents an undoubted threat to the possibility of human excellence. One can thereafter only approach modern society with fear and perhaps trembling and, above all, with caution.

Related to this new view of technology is my reassessment of the truth of modern political philosophy. By modern philosophy I mean the thought that has emerged in western European civilization in the last four or five centuries. Modern philosophy is, more than any other source, responsible for the world we now inhabit. If we are forced to question the goodness of society, we are forced to question the ultimate presuppositions upon which its immediacies depend. Those presuppositions can be seen most clearly in that great line of Western philosophers from Hobbes to Rousseau and from Hegel to Heidegger and Wittgenstein. But if we question these presuppositions, we are driven to look elsewhere for more adequate accounts. The obvious place for a Western man to look is to the Greek philosophers – that is, to the political writings of Plato and Aristotle. In studying these writings, I came to the conclusion that Hegel was not correct in his claim to have taken the truth of antique thought and synthesized it with the modern to produce a higher (and perhaps highest) truth; that on many of the most important political matters Plato's teaching is truer than Hegel's. Particularly, I have come to the conclusion that Plato's account of what constitutes human excellence and the possibility of its realization in the world is more valid than that of Hegel.

I realize the inadequacy of such a brief description of my change of mind. To state quickly why one has changed one's mind is always difficult. Experience and reflection are too intricately bound 'for any ease of intellectual relation.' However, there is no difficulty in expressing my debt to two contemporary thinkers of clarity and, indeed, of genius. Concerning practical questions, I would mention the writings of Jacques Ellul, particularly his book *The Technological Society*. In that work, the structure of modern society is made plain as in nothing else I have read. Concerning the more difficult and more important theoretical questions, my debt is above all to the writings of Leo Strauss. Of Professor Strauss's books I will mention only two: *What is Political Philosophy?*, and *Thoughts on Machiavelli*. As the greatest joy and that most difficult of attainment is any movement of the mind (however small) towards enlightenment, I count it a high blessing to have been acquainted with this man's thought.

George Grant
Hamilton, 1966

Notes

Editor's Introduction

1 B.K. Sandwell, *Saturday Night,* 12 July 1952
2 Grant was later to recant his enthusiasm for Sartre, calling him a clever café atheist and a plagiarist of Heidegger. George Grant, interview by David Cayley, 1985, audiocassette. David Cayley kindly lent me the tapes of those interviews.
3 Robert Fulford, 'The Enemy of Uplift,' Toronto *Star,* 11 November 1959
4 Sydney Harris, 'Our Moral Life' (n.p., n.d.), review of *Philosophy in the Mass Age* found in Grant's papers
5 Grant's many notebooks are, as yet, unpublished. As an interim method of identification Sheila Grant has assigned the notebook for 1956–7 the letter 'I'.
6 George Grant, 'Notebook I,' 39
7 George Grant to Maude Grant, 12 August [1941]
8 George Grant, 'Notebook I,' 39
9 George Grant, 'Adult Education in the Expanding Economy,' *Food for Thought* 15, no. 1 (September–October 1954): 4–10
10 George Grant, 'The Minds of Men in the Atomic Age,' in *Texts Of Addresses Delivered at the 24th Annual Couchiching Conference: August 13th–20th 1955* (Toronto: Canadian Institute on Public Affairs and Canadian Broadcasting Corporation 1955), 39–45

11 Grant, 'Notebook I,' 99
12 Ibid., 86
13 Ibid., 130
14 'What I have to put together is (a) the really open faith which seems to me in Protestantism which can find no set place in the world – the infinite possibility of transcendence once one has made the discovery of subjectivity – Kant a great Protestant and of this I am sure as against Catholicism – the denial of the soul as substance (b) on the other hand since coming to England – the discovery of the world, the importance of sex & economics in shaping the world – historically – put these together. And it is not easy to put these together – because it is just in (a) that I want to escape from cosmological thinking as Jaspers would call it – and here I am at one with people like Wittgenstein, Wisdom, etc. (even here I can accept the [ill] business) on the other hand it is just the living with sex & economics that requires a cosmology. After all Freud and Marx are the most cosmological thinkers & at one & the same time I want to destroy them by an appeal to the transcendent – the mysteries and at the other end I want to learn from them.' George Grant, 'Notebook I,' 29–30
15 Ibid., 31
16 George Grant to his mother, after August 1941
17 George Grant, 'The Paradox of Democratic Education,' *The Bulletin* (published by the Ontario Secondary School Teachers' Federation) 35, no. 6 (November 1955), 275–80 (The Second Ansley Memorial Lecture, delivered on October 1st, 1955 at Assumption University, Windsor)
18 Grant, 'Notebook I,' 13
19 George Grant to Derek Bedson, 1 January 1959
20 George Grant to Derek Bedson, 14 November 1959
21 Grant, 'Notebook I'
22 Grant, 'Notebook 4'
23 George Grant, 'Book review of *The Technological Society* by Jacques Ellul,' *Canadian Dimension* 3, nos. 3, 4 (March–April, May–June), 60
24 George Grant, 'The Case against Abortion,' *Today Magazine*, 3 October 1981, 13

1 Philosophy in the Mass Society

1 In speaking of North American society, I do not wish to imply that there

is no difference between Canada and the United States. I am a firm believer in the idea of British North America. But, for the present purposes, there is no need to make that distinction.

2 Such a statement is, of course, dependent on the supposition that the Roman Catholic Church will never take into itself the truth of freedom which Protestantism knows.

2 The Mythic and Modern Consciousness

1 For what follows about archaic man, I must express my profound dependence on the work of Mircea Eliade. See especially his *The Myth of the Eternal Return* (London: Routledge & Kegan Paul, Ltd. 1955); *Traite d'histoire des religions* (Paris 1953); and *Images et Symboles* (Paris: Gallimard 1952). Professor Eliade seems to me unique among modern scholars of religion not only in his grasp of the facts, but also in his philosophical and theological wisdom.

2 [For a recent description of this see L. Paul, *Nature into History* (London 1958)]

3 [For a recent novel about this see Alejo Carpentier, *The Lost Steps* (n.p., n.d.)]

4 From the foregoing I do not mean in any way to imply that mysticism is an activity appropriate only to archaic cultures. Mysticism, as an explicit doctrine and practice, has in such moderns as St John of the Cross and Jacob Boehme obviously passed beyond the limits of the archaic.

3 Natural Law

1 It is worth noting that George Macdonald was the author of those lovely children's books, *The Princess and the Goblins, Curdie and the Princess,* and *The Back of the North Wind.*

4 History as Progress

1 On this complex and little discussed subject, Michael B. Foster has written two illuminating articles: 'The Christian Doctrine of Creation and the Rise of Modern Natural Science,' *Mind* (October 1934), and 'Christian Theology and the Modern Science of Nature,' *Mind* (October 1935–January 1936).

5 Marxism

1 The difficulty of studying Marx in his own writings must be emphasized. His master work, *Capital*, consciously imitates the structure of Hegel's *Logic*, with its scheme of being, essence, and idea. Also, some of Marx's profoundest thought is to be found in his early writings which are not easily available in English. For instance, his philosophy of history begins to take shape in a magazine article protesting a German law which penalized the collection of firewood by the poor. The reader is therefore advised to approach the study of Marx through such modern commentaries as A. Cornu's *K. Marx et F. Engels*, vol. I (Paris: Presses Universitaires de France 1955), vol. II (Paris: Presses Universitaires de France 1958), and J. Hyppolite's *Etudes sur Marx et Hegel* (Paris: Riviere 1955).

2 It is difficult for English-speaking peoples to admit the spiritual greatness of the Germans. In our last two wars we have been taught to despise their civilization. Nevertheless, the fact remains that the highest European achievements in music and philosophy have come from the Germans. Indeed the ambiguity of German history is that these people have been capable of the most appalling evil, but also of the highest reaches of the human spirit. In western philosophy, for instance, two periods of thought stand out as the most brilliant: the fourth century BC in Greece, which we associate with Plato and Aristotle, and the late eighteenth century in Germany, whose masters were Kant and Hegel. There are no more remarkable books on human history than Hegel's *Philosophy of History* and his *Phenomenology of Mind*. Marx is the heir to this tradition of German philosophical genius. I write about Marx in these essays because his thought is the most influential way that German philosophy has gone out into the world, but under his thought at every point lies the much profounder genius of Hegel.

3 I need hardly stress what a different view this is of man and nature, and their relationship, compared with the Greek view of natural law.

6 The Limits of Progress

1 What follows is not intended to pass as a systematic critique of Marxism, but as the making of one central point.

2 It must be repeated once again that words such as Enlightenment and Reformation are only inadequate shorthand.

3 I am not concerned with the Communist argument that this subordination was necessary if their regimes in Russia and China were to survive against the West and against internal enemies. What I am saying does not rest on the assertion or denial of this historical judgement. The truth of this could only be established by sifting an enormous amount of historical data.

7 American Morality

1 As I can only discuss Calvinism and its Puritan offshoots very shortly, let me recommend two books as introductions to the subject, one by a German, the other by a Canadian. The first is Max Weber's *The Protestant Ethic and the Spirit of Capitalism* (London: Allen & Unwin, Ltd. 1930); the other, by Professor Woodhouse of Toronto, is *Puritanism and Liberty* (Toronto: McClelland & Stewart 1938).
2 The reader is reminded that the last line of the quatrain was not intended by Longfellow to have any Giovannian undertones.
3 This identification of Christianity with practicality by North American Protestants is well illustrated by a quotation from my grandfather. 'Work! Honest work for and with God in Christ! This is the Gospel that is preached unto us. No form, new or old, no pet doctrine or panacea, no institution or catechism can take the place of that.' G.M. Grant to the Synod of the Presbyterian Church in Nova Scotia 1866
4 I have borrowed the example of the judicial condemnation of the innocent from Miss G.E.M. Anscombe's article in *Philosophy* (January 1958).
5 The evidence about the Hiss case is still full of uncertainties. It must be emphasized that in saying this I am not concerned with the arrogance, foolishness, or perversion of Hiss, but whether he was innocent of the crime of which he was convicted, and if so, whether those responsible for his conviction knew of his innocence.
6 The most brilliant modern attempts at such a justification are Kant's *Groundwork of the Metaphysics of Morals* and Hegel's *Philosophy of Right*.

8 Law, Freedom, and Progress

1 [John 21:18]
2 In making such a statement, I must, of course, emphasize that the Roman Catholic Church is in a different position from that of any other ecclesi-

astical body, because of its systematic encouragement of philosophical study among its members. Within its fold, the corpus of tradition is being brought continually before the court of definition, in a way which allows the possibility of a dynamic restatement arising in its midst.

Appendix 2

1 J. Ellul, *The Technological Society* (London: Jonathan Cape 1965, xxxiii